# Ignacy Paderewski

# Ignacy Paderewski
## Poland
Anita Prazmowska

First published in Great Britain in 2009 by
Haus Publishing Ltd
70 Cadogan Place
London SW1X 9AH
*www.hauspublishing.com*

A CIP catalogue record for this book
is available from the British Library

ISBN 978-1-905791-70-5

Series design by Susan Buchanan
Typeset in Sabon by MacGuru Ltd
Printed in Dubai by Oriental Press
Map by Martin Lubikowski, ML Design, London

# Contents

*Introduction: The Polish Question*                                vii

**I The Life and the Land**                                         1
1  Ignacy Paderewski                                                 3
2  Roman Dmowski                                                    18
3  The First World War                                              35

**II The Paris Peace Conference**                                  59
4  The Emergence of Independent Poland                              61
5  Paris                                                            76
6  Unfinished Business                                              98

**III The Legacy**                                                119
7  The Realities of Independent Poland                            121
8  The Return to the Piano                                         140

*Conclusion*                                                      154

*Notes*                                                           160
*Chronology*                                                      168
*Bibliography*                                                    186
*Picture Sources*                                                 191
*Index*                                                           193

# Introduction: The Polish Question

The Polish state did not exist before the outbreak of the First World War. But its absence from the map of Europe was not taken for granted. On the contrary, the 'Polish Question' as it came to be known, was one which politicians, revolutionaries and progressive thinkers alike frequently made pronouncements on. During the second half of the 19th century, when the issue of national self-determination became linked to political reform, it was increasingly accepted that the break-up of the Polish Kingdom had been an injustice. The restoration of Poland was thus not just an issue for the Poles, but was seen as a problem which had wider European implications that would have to be addressed.

The Polish-Lithuanian Commonwealth had been destroyed by three successive Partitions. The first, in 1772, was carried out by Prussia, Austria and Russia. The Second, in 1793, only involved Prussia and Russia. The final one in 1795, signed by all three powers, finished the job by apportioning the remaining territories of what had once been a great Central European state between the signatories. As a result the Commonwealth ceased to exist. Not until 1919, when Poland was restored to the map of Europe as an independent state, did the Poles succeed in reclaiming their independence. By then, however, they had to accept that it would not be possible to bring back the Poland that had existed before Partition. Furthermore, the political turbulence of the 19th century had created new political creeds and with them new forms of governance and political representation.

ooooo

In 1386 Jogaila, the ruler of Lithuania, had married Jadwiga, Queen of Poland, a union which brought under one crown the Kingdom of Poland and the Duchy of Lithuania. In years to come this union was beset by difficulties. But ultimately what kept the Lithuanian and Polish nobility together was the realisation that independently they would not be able to withstand the power of the Teutonic Knights and of the Russian Empire, and in December 1568 representatives of both nobilities decided to transform what was still a personal union into a formal one.

The Polish-Lithuanian Commonwealth was a multi-cultural, multi-faith state spanning the region between Prussia in the west and the Russian Empire in the east, stretching from the Baltic to the Black Sea. By the 18th century, in spite of its control of vast areas, the Commonwealth had become the object of its neighbours' political and territorial aspirations. Internally, the growing power of the nobility, paralleled by the diminishing power of the state led to military weaknesses and finally to its collapse.

In 1572 Zygmund August of the Jagiellonian line, the last hereditary King of the Polish Kingdom and Duchy of Lithuania, died without issue. What happened then was unique in Europe. The nobility assumed the right to choose the next monarch. Henceforth the death or deposition of a king was followed by an election in which all those of noble rank could vote. These elections became international 'fairs' at which foreign princes or their agents vied for the throne of Poland by offering inducements to the noble electorate such as tax exemptions, release from military service and restrictions on the growing power of the merchant classes. In return the nobility sought to bind the prospective monarch to the defence of the interests of the Commonwealth. Though not always disastrously, the Polish-Lithuanian Commonwealth was ruled by a motley succession of elected kings who rarely had the interests of their subjects close to their hearts. The first, Henry, Duke of Anjou, lasted only five months, departing in haste to claim the throne of France. His successor Stefan Batory, Prince of Transylvania, was also the claimant to the Hungarian throne, which meant that wars against the Ottoman Empire took priority over the defence of Polish interests on the Baltic coast. When Batory died in 1586, the next two elected kings were of the Swedish Vasa dynasty. The Commonwealth thus became embroiled in long and ultimately disastrous wars with Sweden. In the meantime the Russian Empire grew in strength, as did the Protestant rulers of Sweden and the German states. The period 1673–96 is associated with the rule of the elected king Jan Sobieski, a time of relative stability though the Commonwealth faced constant conflicts with the Turks. His successor to the Polish throne was the Elector of Saxony. In 1764 Stanisław August Poniatowski, one-time lover of Catherine the Great of Russia, took over as the King of the Polish-Lithuanian Commonwealth. He attempted to introduce reforms which would have strengthened the power of the state and reduced the nobility's privileges. But these measures came too late;

in any case the nobles, hell-bent on defending what they saw as their 'republic', opposed him. By then, the once-powerful Commonwealth was reduced to a pawn in conflicts between the European Powers.

In August 1772 the three neighbouring empires, Prussia, Austria and Russia, agreed to the First Partition. Prussia took Royal Prussia (later East Prussia), Russia gained parts of Belorussia and Livonia, while Austria seized Galicia. France and the Ottoman Empire disapproved but could do little about it. In any event, they were less concerned with the weakening of the Polish-Lithuanian Commonwealth and more with the growth of Russian power. By failing to support the Polish-Lithuanian Commonwealth, however, they missed a chance to reduce the growth of Russian influence in Europe. The Commonwealth lost 30 per cent of its territory, with Russia being the main beneficiary. For Catherine the Great, the territorial acquisitions were outweighed by the fact that henceforth Prussia and Austria accepted Russia's direct interest in the internal affairs of the Commonwealth.

For some of the Polish nobility the shock of the Partition was tempered by the realisation that they could benefit from allying themselves with their Russian rulers. The more enlightened sections of the community, however, began to inquire into the causes of this humiliation. Henceforth a pattern was set. Defeat at the hands of the neighbouring powers was followed by intense debates on the causes of internal weakness and these usually led to attempts to introduce reforms. Failed insurrections led to prolonged periods of soul-searching and a growing awareness that the nobility's political influence had been destroyed. That class could not on its own reverse the political humiliation of the Partition nor could it create national unity. Independence could only be achieved through the introduction of laws abolishing noble privileges and guaranteeing equality.

At the same time, Polish thinkers became only too painfully aware that the survival of the Commonwealth depended on the breaking-up of the coalition of Partition powers. Unfortunately, the outbreak of the French Revolution and general anxiety about the spread of revolutionary ideas in Europe only strengthened the political ties between the three. As Prussia and Austria faced wars with Revolutionary France, they were only too happy to see Russia increase its hold over Poland. In January 1793 Prussia and Russia signed the Second Partition of Poland. Prussia received the town of Toruń, and areas of Masovia and Wielkopolska, while Russia got the Ukraine, Podolia and the remainder of Belorussia. The response of the Polish nobility was confused. Some went into voluntary exile, convinced that the fight against Poland's enemies was best conducted abroad, in particular in France, where the revolutionary government offered the opportunity not only to defeat the Prussians and Austrians but also to destroy the ruling elites and the reactionary political system. Back in Poland Tadeusz Kościuszko (1746–1817) led an insurrection in 1794. A member of an impoverished noble family, Kościuszko had chosen a military career. After the First Partition of Poland he left to seek his fortune in Western Europe. In 1775 he was recruited in France to fight in the American Revolutionary War, where he served with distinction. When he returned to Poland, he was chosen to head the national uprising.

For the first time, the rebels recognised the importance of addressing problems of social inequality, in particular that of serfdom. Unfortunately this first attempt at staging a national uprising was defeated by Russia and resulted in the three neighbouring empires agreeing to the final Third Partition in January 1795, in which Austria took the city of Kraków and areas of Małopolska, Prussia got Warsaw, the areas previously incorporated into Masovia and the Lithuanian territories up to the river Niemen, and Russia absorbed what was left of Lithuania. The Polish-Lithuanian Commonwealth thus ceased to exist. Henceforth the struggle to regain independence was fought in West European capitals, where those who had fought in the uprising fled to escape persecution and in the hope of maintaining international awareness of the injustice of the Partitions. Every European crisis would hereafter be viewed from the perspective of whether it offered an opportunity to break up the consensus between Austria, Prussia and Russia on the Polish question.

The French Revolutionary and Napoleonic Wars offered the greatest hope for the restoration of an independent Poland. But the Poles were not willing to merely wait for the conflict between France and the European powers to weaken Poland's enemies. By various means they sought to make a direct contribution to the French military effort and through that to secure from the French a commitment to their independence. In 1798 a group of Polish exiles in France approached Napoleon Bonaparte with a request for permission to form a Polish Legion which would fight under his command. Bonaparte was only too willing to agree and as a result the Poles fought for France throughout the Napoleonic Wars, even though most of the campaigns in which they served were far from Poland. Their hopes were encouraged by vague promises that France was committed to their country's restoration. In reality, Bonaparte simply wanted to use Polish manpower. After 1805 French victories and the advance east offered more realistic hopes that Polish dreams would be fulfilled. In July 1807 Prussia and Russia made peace with France in the Treaty of Tilsit. The now Emperor Napoleon made a half-hearted effort to pacify the Poles by creating the Duchy of Warsaw, to which territory seized from Austria was later added. This territorial construct was seen as no more than a sop to the wishes of the Poles, who, probably unwisely, had vested great hopes in Napoleon. Nevertheless, when the French army marched east in 1812 in an attempt to conquer Russia, the Poles served yet again. But when the French were defeated, the fate of the Duchy of Warsaw was a foregone conclusion.

In 1814 the European powers, which had defeated Napoleon met in Vienna to discuss the fate of his empire. The fate of the Duchy of Warsaw was decided by the victors. After minor territorial adjustments, it was renamed the Kingdom of Poland and in theory became an independent state, but in reality it became part of the Russian Empire as the Tsar became its king. Although it had been assumed that Congress Poland, as it was commonly known, would be nominally an independent state, successive Tsars had no intention of allowing the Poles to decide their

The Poles went to great lengths to win Napoleon to their cause. Making a military contribution was but one way of making the Emperor feel that he owed a debt of gratitude towards the Poles. The other was providing him with a beautiful Polish mistress when he passed through Polish territory during the war against Russia. The pious Madame Marie Walewska (1786–1817) was prevailed upon to succumb to Napoleon on grounds that it was her patriotic duty to bind him to the Polish cause. In reality Napoleon played a subtle game, establishing the puppet Duchy which fell far short of what the Poles had hoped for. Napoleon needed Polish manpower but was always careful to make sure that Polish units were dispersed and not concentrated on fighting against Russia. This meant that Polish troops served in the Peninsular War and quelled slave uprisings in Haiti. Madame Walewska bore Napoleon a son, though that did not prevent him from later marrying the daughter of the Austrian Emperor.

own fate. Increased Russian control of Congress Poland was once more made possible by the unity of the three victorious empires, Russia, Austria and Prussia. Each ruler had good reason to be anxious about the spread of revolutionary ideas, of which demands for liberal constitutional reforms were the most obvious, the three stood united in their determination to restore the old order. Polish nationalism, which had clearly derived strength from the progressive ideas emanating from France, was thus seen as a disruptive force. This meant that while neither Prussia nor Austria wanted to see the extension of Russian influence into Western Europe, both were only too willing to see the Tsar stamp out Polish nationalism.

Nevertheless, in the years that followed Polish nationalism grew in strength. The Partition Powers each ruled their Polish areas in accordance with their own policies and only came together when an uprising in one area threatened the stability of the others. After the Congress of Vienna, Europe was rocked by violent upheavals. The governments, in spite of their commitment to fighting the spread of liberal ideas, failed to stem the growth of radical revolutionary organisations. Polish political exiles, motivated by the belief that the collapse of the old regimes would ultimately benefit their cause, participated in revolutions wherever they happened to take place, be it Paris, Vienna or Piedmont. At the same time, in the former Polish territories the fight against foreign domination continued. The November Uprising in 1830 and the January Uprising in 1863 were the most famous insurrections, but undoubtedly also the most damaging to the Polish cause as both disastrously failed to force the Russians out.

The 1830 November Uprising was started by young army officers. Most had belonged to secret societies and Masonic Lodges which flourished among university students and the officer corps. The older generation on the whole felt uneasy about the young men's plans and in fact did not initially support the fighting that broke out in the streets of Warsaw on the evening of 29 November 1830. An attempt to assassinate the Tsar's brother failed but fighting against Russian troops stationed in Warsaw spread. Somewhat optimistically, the young men felt that the international situation was in their favour as the July Revolution in Paris and similar events in Belgium suggested that progressive forces, ones likely to support the Poles' right to self-determination, were gaining the upper hand in Western Europe. When the Sejm (the Polish constituent assembly which the Russians initially tolerated), inspired by the initial successes against the Russian units in Warsaw, declared Poland to be independent, Tsar Nicolas I authorised military action. By May 1832 the uprising was defeated and brutal reprisals followed. The insurrectionists' hopes that Prussia would take advantage of Russia's difficulties and perhaps help them proved incorrect. France and Britain confined themselves to expressing moral support but did nothing to hinder Russian reprisals. Critically, the assumption that all Poles would respond to the news of the attempted assassination of the Tsar's brother by staging a mass uprising proved to be false. The peasant community remained indifferent, as did most townspeople.

During the revolutionary upsurge in Europe of 1848–9, Poles once more hoped that the international situation was volatile enough to allow another bid for freedom. In many European capitals Polish exiles fought for constitutional reform and the extension of voting rights, even though these had nothing to do with the Polish question. Their assumption that governments established on the basis of true representation would automatically be supportive of their demand for the restoration of a Polish state turned out to be wrong. German and Austrian liberals turned out to be just as unwilling to consider freedom for the Poles as the conservatives had been.

During the Crimean War (1853–6) the Polish question was again forced onto the international agenda, this time due to the Ottoman Empire's willingness to take up the Polish cause in the hope of weakening Russia. The Ottoman Empire had earlier given refuge to political exiles who had fled from Poland after the 1848–9 revolutions. During the Crimean War these men attempted to make a direct contribution to the Ottoman war effort in order to ensure that the restoration of Poland became one of its war aims. When the war ended, however, this did not happen. None of the European powers, least of all the Ottomans, wanted to prolong the conflict with Russia and the Polish issue was dropped.

In January 1863 a national uprising broke out in Russian Poland. More than ever before, the rebels linked the question of national independence to political reforms. They planned not only to overthrow Russian dominance and to unite all Polish areas but also to address the thorny issues of serfdom and the emancipation of the Jews. If they were highly aware of the need to ensure that this was a truly national uprising, they were just as acutely aware of the need to secure international support. Initially it looked as if they had succeeded. When Russian troops were sent into action in Polish areas, the British, French and Austrian governments all protested. The Vatican, mindful of the fact that capital could be gained from taking up the cause of the Catholic Poles in their fight against the Orthodox Russian government, protested vigorously. But verbal protests were all that there were. Ultimately Russia was left to suppress the insurrection by force, while

Prussia assured the Russians that it would not interfere. Otto von Bismarck, the Prussian Prime Minister, had no intention of encouraging the Poles; on the contrary, he was committed to integrating his Polish subjects more closely into Prussia. When the uprising collapsed, Russian retaliation was predictably brutal. All remaining vestiges of Polish autonomy within Congress Poland were eradicated and a process of Russification, aimed at destroying the Polish language and culture, began.

Over the years, in spite of each of the Partition Powers governing the Polish areas under their control, according to their own policies, a sense of Polish national awareness developed. In territories under Prussian administration a policy of Germanisation was introduced, aimed at eradicating all evidence of Polish culture. The Prussian state provided funds to encourage German colonisation by buying up Polish land. This had the unexpected result of forcing Polish peasants to improve their output and thus led to a higher standard of agriculture. By contrast, Congress Poland, industrialised, benefiting from integration into the vast Russian Empire. The opposite picture was presented by areas under Austrian control, where the political rights of the Polish community were guaranteed by the establishment of local assemblies, but at the same time they were neglected economically. Rural life dominated by the local landowners continued to be the norm in Austrian Poland. Although it was possible to speak of a common Polish language and culture, there was no such thing as a single Polish economy, as each area developed differently. These differences led to the emergence of new ideas on whether and in what way Poland could regain its independence. Among the Polish nobility in the Austrian and Russian areas, as well as the industrialists and entrepreneurs of the Russian areas, there were those who called for the end of talk about uprisings, instead suggesting that economic wellbeing and political stability would go hand-in-hand and that Poles stood to gain more from co-operation with the Partition governments. Towards the end of the 19th century the emerging Socialist movement and the newly-established Nationalist movement agreed on the importance of pursuing economic and political reforms, though the latter demanded that all efforts should be focused on the defence of the nation, thus subordinating political reforms to the fight for independence. Polish Socialists, in particular those from the politically repressive Russian Empire, saw the revolution as being a priority while still disagreeing among themselves as to whether the fight for an independent Poland was of any importance to the Socialist cause. The fact that Karl Marx and the First International condemned the Partition of Poland gave the impression that the European labour movement was likely to support the Poles in their quest for independence.

The destruction of the Polish Kingdom and the successive failures to reverse this tragedy led to the development of a particular Polish view of its history and coloured its cultural life. Daily life was dominated by a sense of loss and a struggle to maintain native culture. This meant that literature, music and painting were overlaid with images which looked back to the days of independence, while the future was seen through a deeply pessimistic prism. During the second half of the 19th century Classicism gave way to Romanticism and what some have defined as Polish Romanticism. This was particularly the case with poetry. Adam Mickewicz (1798–1855) and Juliusz Słowacki (1809–49) are the best examples of this style, which was imbued with pathos, pain and longing, through being inextricably connected with the dilemmas generated by the national tragedy. Both writers and painters felt the need to reassess the past. The past had become the single most important inspiration both to those who desired to seek an explanation as to why Poland was subjugated but also as an inspiration and as encouragement. If the Polish Kingdom did not exist, the existence of the Polish nation was being reaffirmed through works which reviewed its great historic moments. Among writers, the most prominent exponent of this was Henryk Sienkiewicz (1846–1916) whose momentous historical novels focused on the great events and battles of the past. In the process, the nobility and its exploits were offered as an expression of true Polish identity. Never mind that in the process the truth became simplified and complexities were lost, Sienkiewicz aimed to inspire the young with a conviction that through great deeds the true character of the nation had been moulded.

In the visual arts no painter exceeded the output of Jan Matejko (1838–93), whose canvases left little to the imagination. They portrayed battles and events in which good was pitched against evil and Polish greatness prevailed. The size of his paintings and the drama which they conveyed were intended to commemorate key stages in history, as much as condemn those who betrayed the nation. Artur Grottger (1837–67) produced paintings of a different style, distinctly melancholy, wringing every last tear out of the viewer's eye with their portrayal of the cost of the failed January Uprising. Exile and loss dominated his canvases.

Towards the end of the 19th century this preoccupation with the nation's tragedies, the glorification of the republic of the gentry and use of the past to maintain national spirit came into conflict with new trends, those which recognised the great historic changes caused by industrialisation and the emergence of influential new social groups. Proponents of these ideas wanted to focus on educational reforms, social improvement, alleviating rural poverty and on the implications of industrialisation. The writings of Stefan Żeromski (1864–1925) focused on the consequences of industrialisation and on the failures of the insurrections and the price paid by the people. He and other writers liked to portray the peasant community as the true heart of the nation, suggesting that the nobility was concerned only with itself. Others identified the workers as the noble men of toil. In all cases what was striking was the extent to which history and the national question dominated artistic expression, apparently demanding that each artist focus on those issues as the main purpose of creative endeavour.

In Polish areas under Russian control, and in particular after the January Uprising when Russian repression was particularly severe, there was no public forum for cultural expression. Instead concerts, poetry readings and theatrical performances took place in private houses; the piano pieces and dances of Frederik Chopin (1810–48) being particularly appropriate. In any case, Russian censorship affected not only printed works, but also musical performances. Russian censors rightly saw all forms of creativity as an attempt to maintain a sense of national identity and cohesion which transcended the boundaries of the three Empires. At the same time the highly-politicised communities of Polish exiles in the West maintained links with their countrymen living under foreign rule.

On the night of 8/9 February 1904 the Japanese attacked the Russian naval base at Port Arthur, on the coast of Manchuria. In the war which followed the Russian fleet was defeated and the Empire humiliated by the first Asiatic state to defeat a European power. This led to internal disturbances, during which rural and urban conflicts increased. Tsar Nicholas II was reluctantly persuaded to end the war with Japan so that the army could be used to deal with this instability which also affected the Polish areas. On 5 September 1905 the war was ended by the signing of the Treaty of Portsmouth, Japan dictating humiliating conditions to the Russians. The Poles saw the Russo-Japanese conflict and the public exposure of the Russian Empire's impotence as the moment they had been waiting for, and two Polish Nationalist leaders, Roman Dmowski and Józef Piłsudski actually went to Tokyo in search of Japanese support, but with no success (see Chapter 3).

The next European crisis which appeared to offer an opportunity to the Poles came in 1908 when Austria-Hungary occupied Bosnia and Hercegovina, thus exacerbating the tense situation in the Balkans. The Ottoman Empire was particularly concerned, seeing this as an open attack on its own weakening position in the area, but Britain, France and the Russian Empire also kept an eye on developments in the Balkans. The Austrian move, at first glance of minor significance, in fact indicated the possibility of a renewed European power struggle, at the root of which was the fact that the Ottomans were being pushed out of Europe. The scene looked set for another international conflict from which the Poles could benefit, and this time they were better prepared to take advantage of the collapse of the existing European balance of power. The Polish conspiratorial organisations and leaders had absorbed the lessons of the previous national uprisings and believed that they now knew how they could take advantage of a breakdown in the international European consensus to secure Poland's independence.

In the Russian- and German-held areas, where anti-Polish

policies were most repressive, the call to prepare for the coming fight ahead was eagerly heeded. In the three empires various Polish political parties had emerged. These now put forward proposals for how independence could be secured and what form the new state should take. Those who believed that the three Partition regimes could be persuaded to grant the Poles autonomy clashed with those who pointed to increasing rather than weakening repression and called for preparations for military action. Roman Dmowski's National Democratic Party gained most support before 1914, while the Socialists and the Peasant Party held their own.

After 1908 Dmowski advocated reconciliation between the Poles and Russians, reasoning that Germany posed the greatest threat to Polish nationalism. Piłsudski, on the other hand, took a different view. He reasoned that the Poles should in the first place prepare to fight for independence and that this would be won through making a direct military contribution to the much-anticipated European war. Both leaders observed the international situation keenly, waiting for an opportunity which the Poles could exploit to their advantage. In 1914 there was no indication, however, that any of the three empires would voluntarily relinquish their Polish territories and that they would tolerate the restoration of Poland to the map of Europe. Thus all plans for a Polish state were formulated on the assumption that the existing international balance of power had to collapse.

Ignacy Jan Paderewski, pianist of international renown. His main repertoire included Chopin and Liszt. Polish delegate to the Paris Peace talks. Before the outbreak of the war he was associated with Polish exile groups campaigning for the restoration of Poland. The outbreak of the war led to his abandonment of his musical career and focus on highlighting the Polish case, mainly in the United States. On his arrival in Paris in April 1920 he could count on securing the support of the international statesmen for Poland's aspirations, as he knew most of them personally and was very much socially at ease in the Paris salons.

# I

# The Life and the Land

# 1
## Ignacy Paderewski

Ignacy Jan Paderewski was born on 6 November 1860 in the provincial town of Kuryłówka in Podolia. The region had initially belonged to the Duchy of Lithuania but had then been taken over by the Polish Kingdom. During the Partitions Podolia had been divided between Russia and Austria. Paderewski was thus born and brought up under Russian rule. His father was an estate administrator, and his mother died soon after giving birth to her only son. The Podolia region had always been inhabited by a mixed population. While the large landed estates were usually owned by Poles, the local rural population was mainly Ukrainian, while in the small towns the Jewish community predominated, in some cases making up more than 50 per cent of the population.

Until his departure for Warsaw at the tender age of 12 to study at the Music Institute, young Ignacy was tutored at home. Within the narrow confines of the Polish landlord community in which his father mixed, the traumas of the collapse of the January Uprising of 1863 and the Russian repression which followed were still felt. The general atmosphere of gloom and despondency was difficult to avoid. Ignacy's father, accused of having aided the insurrection, had been imprisoned for a year. But his experience was not unusual and in fact he had got off lightly. Many local men had been sent to Siberia for involvement in the insurrection. The sense of national tragedy was undoubtedly encouraged by the fact that his tutor Babinski had taken part in the November 1830 uprising and had had to go into exile in the West. When he returned to Poland in 1868 Ignacy's father employed him.

Ignacy's musical training until then had been far from satisfactory. In years to come he wrote; *My first teacher, the violin player Runowski, knew nothing about the technique of the piano. Sowiński, who succeeded him, was not very well acquainted either with piano technique, so he could not teach me anything. One was as bad as the other.*[2] Babinski taught Ignacy Polish and French, and provided him with rigorous music lessons. The atmosphere at home was imbued with patriotic feelings which were maintained and encouraged by the children and young people being constantly reminded of the great events of the past, when the Polish Kingdom ruled Central Europe. In 1870 hopes were briefly raised of an imminent reversal of Poland's fortunes when Prussia and France went to war. At that time it was generally believed that France was Poland's ally and that the defeat of Prussia would break the consensus between the three Partition Powers. This of course did not happen because Prussia defeated France.

In 1872 Ignacy was enrolled in the Music Institute in

'When I was three years old I began to play with one finger, with one small finger I tried to find the melodies – and when I was four, I began then to use all my fingers. So after I had attained my fourth year, I possessed that much musicianship.'
**IGNACY PADEREWSKI**[1]

Warsaw. In spite of his tender age, he already had a very high opinion of his musical abilities. In a provincial small town the musically-gifted boy was encouraged to believe that he was destined for greater things. This was an opinion with which few of his tutors agreed, however, detecting in the first place lack of technique and application. Ignacy proved to be a difficult student and indeed on one occasion he was expelled for insubordination. He would have preferred to study abroad, possibly in Vienna or Berlin, but his father refused to pay for it. While still a high school pupil he tried without success to form a concert group. When this failed, with ill grace he returned to the Institute to complete his education. At the age of only 20 he met and married Antonina Korsakówna, who died a year later, ten days after giving birth to a son Alfred, Paderewski's only child. Tragically he was disabled, and died in his early twenties. It has been suggested that these personal tragedies freed Paderewski to pursue his studies and career further afield, something he might not have done had his wife lived, requiring him to support her and their child.[3] Initially Paderewski left his son with his father. In 1885, when his father became frail, Paderewski brought his son to Paris where he left him in the care of the Górski family.

At this stage Paderewski was still undecided about his future career. On the one hand he was working towards becoming a pianist, but he also had aspirations to compose. His first period of study abroad was in Berlin, a city which he came to dislike, not least because his stay there coincided with Prussia's growing determination to integrate the Polish community into German life. Any signs of Polish cultural self-expression were disapproved of. But in Vienna, where he moved in 1884, Paderewski felt more at home. Here he was enrolled as a student with the famous piano teacher

Theodor Leschetizky, best known for having pioneered the modern technique of piano playing; Leschetizky was the link between 20th-century piano playing and the Romantic school of Chopin and Liszt. The city's cultural atmosphere suited Paderewski. He met some of the famous European composers and musical virtuosi, notably Johannes Brahms. Furthermore, the Austrian attitude towards the Polish question was more relaxed. In the Austro-Hungarian Empire prominent Polish politicians were able to openly discuss the relative merits of Poles seeking autonomy within the Empire as opposed to outright independence. The Polish language was not banned and Polish publications were freely available. This was very different from the harshly repressive atmosphere in the Russian and German Partition areas.

In 1888 Paderewski gave concerts in Paris and two years later in London. His audience and critics praised him for his playing, though he himself still hoped to make a mark as a composer. As his career as a pianist took off, his repertoire included compositions by Schubert, Chopin, Rubinstein and Liszt. During frequent trips back to Poland, Paderewski became associated with musicians and poets who looked to folk art for inspiration, thus consolidating his connections with Polish culture. His own compositions were based on those models and fitted into the late Romantic tradition which was so popular among Poles at that time. His biographer described how, 'Paderewski refused to follow the general trend. It should be noted that in his early compositions, this pianist and composer had no thought of virtuoso effects; in his concept the piano was simply to sing the melodies conceived in his soul.'[4]

After his first concert in Paris in February 1888 Paderewski was in constant demand. Not only was he invited to play in the salons of the European nobility but he was repeatedly invited to perform in public. In 1889 he toured France, Romania, Switzerland and Germany. From then on the pattern of his life was set.[5] Brief periods of respite during which he prepared new programmes were followed by months of travel. The scale of his earnings was legendary.

At the height of Paderewski's career, before the First World War, an interesting metamorphosis took place. Although by then he was an extremely well known pianist and a respected composer, he increasingly was seen as a famous Pole. This international profile, even though Poland as a state did not exist, was in itself a gauntlet thrown to the Russian authorities. In his concert programmes he always endeavoured to include the works of Chopin or Moniuszko. Paderewski made it clear that Polish history and folk music, as well as the countryside were his inspirations. He came to symbolise the angst and pain of the Polish nation, a role which he assumed willingly. Significant in his self-appointed role as an ambassador of the Polish cause was the fact that women found his playing particularly interesting.

From being a rebellious and difficult teenager Paderewski had grown into a handsome man. He was not tall, but had a lean muscular frame. The most striking feature was his hair which has been described as a mane. Most noticed its colour which was copper but not quite red. Even in his later years when he had gone grey, his wild but attractive crown of hair attracted attention. His eyes were always piercing and his gaze precise. His manner was courteous and rather old-fashioned which endeared him to women. During his visit to London in May 1890 he met a number of painters who belonged to the Pre-Raphaelite movement, notably Edward Burne-Jones who saw in Paderewski the perfection of male beauty.[6] His romantic aura, brooding presence and flamboyant hairstyle all drew female fans, who flocked in great numbers to his concerts, finding his choice of music and his emotional engagement with what he was playing appealing. It has been suggested that Paderewski cultivated this image, realising that if he wanted the audience to make a link between his musical offerings and the Polish cause, to which he was wholly committed, then he needed to cast himself in the romantic mould which the wider European community expected of Polish patriots.

It is interesting to speculate as to when and why Paderewski made the connection between his skills as a virtuoso pianist and composer on the one hand and the political mission to which he was to dedicate himself wholeheartedly throughout his life on the other. While he had always understood the importance of using music as a means of reminding his listeners of Poland's sufferings, it is difficult to pinpoint when, and indeed whether, he consciously assumed the role of ambassador of the cause. It has been suggested that Paderewski was late in coming to understand that his popularity and the access to the political and social elites which music gave him could be used to win support for Polish independence.

In 1890 Paderewski made his first tour of Britain. The reception from audiences and critics was as good as in any other European capital, though possibly more critical. Nevertheless what made a difference was that Mrs Dallas-Yorke and her sister Lady Barringdon, wife of the secretary of the then Prime Minister Lord Salisbury, were enraptured by his playing and introduced him to London's top social circles. In years to come he would visit England on a regular basis and this allowed him to maintain and extend his circle of influential friends. The late Victorian aristocratic milieu to which

Paderewski was introduced consisted as much of present and future politicians as it did of artists and their patrons. A J Balfour, later to become Lord Balfour, was the first of such acquaintances. At the time Balfour was Chief Secretary for Ireland in the government of his uncle Lord Salisbury. Balfour was the coming man, and in the long term he turned out to be a valuable person to know. In 1891 Balfour became First Lord of the Treasury and in 1898, while his uncle was ill, he took increasing responsibility for foreign affairs. From 1902 to 1905 he was Prime Minister. In 1891 Paderewski also met H H Asquith, who became Prime Minister in 1909. One of his supporters and admirers was Jennie Churchill, mother of Winston Churchill. What were initially social contacts became friendships and Paderewski visited Asquith and Balfour whenever he was in England.

Paderewski was only too well aware that Poles would not be able to secure independence without a profound change in the existing pattern of international relations in Europe. To prepare for independence in the future, an understanding of the European balance of power was required. He was intrigued and fascinated by Britain. His explanation for his inquisitiveness was that *I was always studying the conditions of my own country, and consequently of other countries in relation to mine.*[7] He thus tried to understand the British political system in which, impressively, politicians of the governing party as well as those in opposition shared the same values and treated each other with respect. Undoubtedly, Paderewski was wondering how Poland would be governed were it to emerge as an independent state in the future.

The artistic community was no less enamoured of him. The artists Edward Burne-Jones and Lawrence Alma-Tadema both admired him and painted his portrait. Of the newspaper proprietors whom Paderewski met and with whom he remained in contact throughout his life the most influential was Alfred Harmsworth, owner of the *Daily Mail*. In 1908 Harmsworth, by then Lord Northcliffe, acquired *The Times*. Paderewski's reception in London and the important contacts he made there had immense implications for his assessment of what he could achieve. In London, for the first time, he was greeted not merely as a pianist, but as a representative of the Polish cause. If the first could be used to further the second, Paderewski had decided to make the most of that opportunity.[8] In years to come Paderewski was to say: *Life was at its richest and highest then. It was a great flowering of that English civilization. That I had some little part of that life and great enjoyment in it, is still a spiritual solace to me.*[9]

The desire for professional advancement, and of course financial considerations, were factors in Paderewski's decision to tour the United States. It is however, possible to speculate that his desire to extend his political activities also played a role. During the last decade of the 19th century the United States still showed little inclination to become a player in European affairs, but its economic and accompanying political power could not be ignored. Although it would still be a few years before the United States government could be persuaded that affairs in Europe had a direct impact on its own standing in the world, all European statesmen were only too aware that it was important to look across the Atlantic and to gauge what was happening there. Paderewski might have been initially motivated by a desire to conquer the United States artistically, but he must also have hoped to mobilise the Polish community there to support the fight for an independent Poland.

Paderewski's first and all his subsequent visits to the United States were extremely successful. His musical successes there have been explained by many factors, not all relating to his choice of music or the quality of his performance. To start with the piano manufacturer Steinway & Sons decided to sponsor his trip. In a way that was still novel in the world of classical music, in particular in Europe, Paderewski was tied into an exclusive contract with Steinway. While his accommodation and travel costs were paid by the piano company, during his first tour in 1891 he was obliged to play over 80 performances, only on Steinway pianos. His sponsors dealt with publicity and advertising. The result was a breakneck train tour of the United States. The audience was considerably wider than that at concerts in Europe. These were usually people who had made their own money and wanted to attend events which would confirm their social status. The predominance of women in the audience was striking, as was their behaviour. Many, captivated by Paderewski's playing, wanted to have something to remember him by and he was frequently mobbed after concerts. His fans, for that was what they were, usually tried to cut a lock of his now famous mane of blond hair. For the first time ever, Paderewski needed to be protected from his admirers. He himself was not put off by the fact that classical music was drawing wider audiences. He certainly enjoyed the financial security which these successes brought with them. But he also appears to have appreciated confounding musical critics in Europe, where appreciation of classical music was still confined to relatively small, elitist audiences. In the United States the audiences rather than the critics determined a musician's success, and there his concerts met with popular acclaim.

He became famous and to his satisfaction he was seen as

'the world's most famous Pole'. Before the outbreak of the First World War Paderewski made ten trips to the United States. For each he secured higher payment than any other musician before him had ever obtained. In the United States Paderewski noted greater egalitarianism than in Europe and with that also a commitment to charitable causes. He already knew the writer Henry James whom he had met earlier in London, but Mark Twain became his friend too. The rich and famous, including the Rockefellers, the Carnegies and Gilders, who established the famous Gilder Lehman Institute, welcomed him and from them he learned of the educational establishments and foundations which they supported with their wealth. During his second trip to the United States Paderewski met Joseph Pulitzer, with whom he remained in contact. During his third tour of the United States he befriended Herbert Hoover, then a young student at Stanford University. When Paderewski went to the United States in 1907 he was invited to play for President Theodore Roosevelt at the White House. Although Paderewski was prone to judging his listeners mainly on the basis of their understanding of music, he also was interested to note the extent to which Roosevelt understood developments outside the United States. Paderewski was also gratified to learn that the President of the United States was a keen reader of the Polish author Henryk Sienkiewicz. Although he was an iconic writer for many Poles, it was most unusual for a foreigner to be familiar with his works. In his memoirs Paderewski noted that *certain opinions about my country expressed by President Roosevelt were extremely encouraging to me, and I still gladly and gratefully remember every word*

> 'His mastery of melodious tones is the soul of his achievement.'
>
> *NEW YORK TIMES,* 8 JANUARY 1893

*he said on that subject.*[10] It is safe to assume that President Roosevelt expressed support for Polish independence.

In May 1899 Paderewski married Helena Górska, whom he had met in 1878 when she was married to a close friend and fellow musician. When Paderewski settled in Paris in the 1890s they looked after his young son Alfred. In due course Paderewski fell in love with Helena and her husband withdrew from the scene. When an annulment was obtained from the Catholic Church Paderewski was able to marry her, but Helena was never his only love interest. In fact, during his early days in the West European capitals he had an affair with Princess Rachel de Brancovan of Wallachia, by all accounts a passionate and intriguing woman. It was also rumoured that during one of his trips to the United States he stopped *en route* in Havana where he met and had a dalliance with the famous Russian ballerina Anna Pavlova. Nevertheless, Helena had cared for his son and seems to have easily slipped into a similar caring role in relation to Paderewski himself, who was of a nervous disposition and needed a lot of emotional support. At this time he purchased a house in Switzerland which became his principal residence.

In spite of his successes as a performer, Paderewski really wanted to be a composer. He enjoyed playing; yet, the punishing schedule of tours was merely a means of acquiring sufficient funds to allow him to return to composing.[11] This he tried to do after he acquired his vast house in Switzerland in 1903, where he completed his only opera *Manru* and the Piano Sonata in E flat minor (Ops. 21). Although the opera was very well received its fame did not endure. Its success was put down to the reputation of its composer rather than its intrinsic quality. In 1907 Paderewski completed a symphony. Although widely admired, this and other works are seen as too closely based on Chopin's work. Paderewski had become the great interpreter of Chopin's works but was unable to follow his master. It would seem as if the patriotic message and the obvious parable of suffering and doom were not subjects that Paderewski could convey with any real musical finesse. Unfortunately it was his desire to use music as a medium through which to convey the image of the suffering fatherland and of the great tragedy which had befallen Poland that stood in the way of his composition. In comparison with Chopin, whose music conveyed a romantic mood, Paderewski's compositions told a tale of suffering which did not make them easy or enjoyable listening.

**Frederik Chopin (1810–48)** showed early promise as a pianist and composer. His output is an outstanding example of the Polish romantic style. His music is highly expressive and strongly rooted in the rhythms of Polish folk music. Although Chopin left Poland in 1830 his compositions are considered to be Polish in character, making references to life in the country and to music heard there. However, his salon pieces for the piano also made allusions to other forms of contemporary music, such as *bel canto* opera. At a time when the modern piano had just entered the concert hall and the middle-class home, Chopin and later Liszt were enormously influential in popularising its music.

Throughout his life Paderewski supported many charitable causes, not all of which were connected with Poland. He was the initiator of two major projects, the monument commemorating the victory of the Polish and Lithuanian Commonwealth against the Crusader Knights in 1410 and the monument to the great Polish poet Adam Mickewicz. However, his eagerness to associate with commemorations and anniversaries linked to Poland's great past contrasted with his lack of knowledge of contemporary politics. In reality, although Paderewski was only too willing and indeed able to make a gesture of great pathos, he did not participate in the political life of any of the three Partition areas. In fact his public pronouncements lacked political awareness and were merely rhetoric. Poles nevertheless loved him, although many politicians winced at his naivety and his constant use of outdated romantic imagery.

It was during his tours to the United States that Paderewski made many donations for the benefit of the Polish community there. These included hospitals, libraries and relief funds, all very much appreciated by the Poles, who remained among the poorest of the immigrant communities. He became famous for his willingness to support charitable causes and frequently did so on the spur of the moment. An example of this was a concert he gave at the University of Stanford in 1896 at the request of a group of students. They had asked that the proceeds be donated to charitable causes, to which Paderewski agreed. In years to come Paderewski was reminded by Herbert Hoover that he had been the organiser of the concert.[12] In the United States he played at benefit concerts and frequently waved his usual fee if the cause appealed to him. All this contributed to his image as the 'Greatest Living Pole'. His own conviction that he represented the Polish cause, and the connection which he intentionally made between it and his music, meant that although he was not linked to any particular party in Poland, many believed that he represented the country and its cause and thus expected him to act accordingly.

In the years before the First World War Paderewski's international reputation was tarnished somewhat by the perception that he supported Roman Dmowski, the leader of the nationalist movement in Poland. Although Paderewski always maintained that he had no direct link or association with his movement, by the time he fully understood the implications of Dmowski's political programme and tried to make it clear that he did not, the damage had been done. Dmowski had been a frequent visitor to Paderewski's home in Switzerland and it is likely that the pianist's view of what was happening in Russian Poland came directly from him. Dmowski saw the Jews as enemies of the Polish nation and while committed to the fight for Polish independence, the Jews were the main target of his attacks. In 1912 Paderewski provided Dmowski with funds, ostensibly to help with his campaign for election to the Russian Duma. This money, which was a considerable sum, was in fact used by the National Democrats to publish an anti-Semitic newspaper. At the same time, Dmowski and his collaborators called for a boycott of Jewish businesses, to break what they believed to be the Jewish stranglehold on Polish life.

Paderewski claimed to have found out about this newspaper by accident. Sometime in 1912 an unexpected visitor from Poland called on him in London and gave him a large box containing copies of all editions of the newspaper, which had been published thanks to Paderewski's generosity. Paderewski stated emphatically that he did not share the National Democrats' anti-Semitic views but believed he could do nothing about what had already happened as this would merely increase the tension between Poles and Jews. Even though he was asked by respected members of the Warsaw Jewish community to publicly dissociate himself from the publication, he refused to do so.[13] His memoirs bear witness to the fact that he felt that the conflict between the Jewish and Polish communities was stirred up by the Russian authorities, but still he felt that the Jews had been imprudent and had in effect brought their problems upon themselves.[14] Only when he toured the United States in 1913 was he to realise that the Jewish community there had mobilised against him for maintaining this view. Things became so serious that Paderewski had to be given a police escort. In the end he was advised to make a sworn deposition before a lawyer, which he duly did. *Ignacy Jan Paderewski, being first duly sworn, deposes and says: That I never gave money to any anti-Jewish newspaper whatsoever ... That I never initiated or supported the boycotting of the Jewish trade in Poland, being entirely out of, and not taking any part in active politics in Poland.*[15] Unfortunately for Paderewski, this did not have the desired result and the suspicion that the famous pianist had links with the anti-Semitic National Democrats in Poland persisted.

During the 1913 tour of the United States Paderewski succumbed to what seem to have been panic attacks. This had happened before, and the past he had dealt with the problem by taking some time away from touring. But in the United States the tension caused by the accusations of anti-Semitism, and inflammation of the nerves in his arms made him long for a rest. He stayed briefly in Paso Robles near San Francisco where he discovered mud baths which helped him overcome the inflammation of the nerves. It was clear that Paderewski had come to the point where touring and performing gave him little pleasure and was in fact the cause of extreme pain. Whether a man so used to public adulation and to being the object of international attention would be satisfied to merely settle down to composing was doubtful from the start. When Paderewski returned to Switzerland in 1914 the international situation was tense. A sense of menace and anticipation hung in the air.

# 2

# Roman Dmowski

Roman Dmowski, who was the other Polish signatory to the Versailles Treaty, was very different from the flamboyant, romantic stereotype of a Pole presented by Paderewski. Dmowski was a far darker, more earnest and intense man. Nevertheless, the two men's characters and their desire to serve the Polish cause were moulded by similar events, namely the collapse of the 1863 uprising and the soul-searching which followed. The Russian policy of destroying Polish culture also played a formative role in both their lives.

Dmowski's parents claimed noble origin. His paternal grandfather came from a minor gentry family in the Podlasie region. Their modest estate had been destroyed by French troops during the Napoleonic Wars. The family seems to have been further hit by the territorial redistribution after the defeat of Napoleon. This led Dmowski's father to settle near Warsaw where he married a daughter of a tradesman. Her family too had belonged to the impoverished gentry, though at some time during the 18th century they had been stripped of their noble rank and of their fiscal privileges because of their involvement in manufacturing, in their case tanning. In

August 1864, when Roman Dmowski was born, the family had no links with the gentry. His father had settled in a small town near the Warsaw suburb of Praga where he first worked as a paver and later built up a workshop. The family's economic situation was precarious though both parents were sensitive to the fact that they were of noble origins and transmitted this awareness to their children.[1]

Dmowski's parents had seven children, two of whom died in infancy and two in early adulthood. Dmowski's father had aspirations for his children and the three sons went to secondary school, though Roman was the only one to complete his secondary education and receive the matriculation certificate. A major disincentive to staying at school was the fact that the secondary school attended by the three Dmowski brothers adopted a strict regime and was committed to the policy of Russification which was enforced with particular severity after 1879. To start with young Roman showed little aptitude for learning, by his own admission being 'a little hooligan',[3] and he had to repeat the second, third and fourth grades. Only in the fourth year did Roman show any degree of personal commitment to education, but unfortunately this coincided with his father's tragic death from gangrene in 1884. Had he agreed to an amputation he would have lived, though this was something he refused to consider.

> 'I am a Pole – therefore my whole extended spiritual life I share with Poland's life, its emotions, its thoughts, its need, its aims and aspirations.'
> ROMAN DMOWSKI[2]

Dmowski's first involvement in politics came while he was still at secondary school, when he joined a youth group. In the areas under Russian control all organisations were illegal and the authorities were determined to root out any signs of political activism within the student community. This seemingly innocent association put Dmowski and his friends in considerable danger. The name which the young conspirators adopted was 'The Watchtower'. Their aim was to protect Polish youth from Russification by studying Polish history, literatures and politics. A schoolfriend recalled that 'politically we were all … uniformly determined, in opposition, ready for action'.[4] This was the natural reaction of young Poles to Russian oppression. It was then that Dmowski put forward what were to become later the key principles of his nationalist theory. He firmly believed that Russia was the enemy of Polish nationalism and that Jews had no claim to a Polish identity. He thus opposed the admission of Jewish students into their clandestine organisation and was already critical of those who had social contacts with Jews. In 1886 Dmowski enrolled at the University of Warsaw to study biology. He believed it was important to study a subject that had relevance to the national cause. This idea was in line with the positivist and scientific theories which had replaced discussions about the failed national uprising. Those who professed these new ideas argued that people should be useful and that practical solutions should replace the preoccupation with past glories. Dmowski was particularly successful in his biological studies and was awarded the equivalent of a doctorate.

While his university studies brought him academic success, at the same time Dmowski laid the foundations of his future political career. He joined a youth organisation known as ZET. Although its aim was to bring together various émigré organisations with those in occupied Poland to focus the Poles' efforts on a common purpose, Dmowski had his own ideas. He became one of the leading lights within the Warsaw branch and through it started implementing his own vision of what the organisation and its objectives should be. He wanted it to focus entirely on the Polish cause and to distance itself from Socialist organisations which he saw as lacking in commitment to Polish nationalism. His first initiative was to expel Socialists from the ZET. He succeeded because he rightly concluded that Polish students' primary loyalty was to Poland and not to other students: 'The purge of the Warsaw youth organisations was not achieved by the nationalist movement. With few notable exceptions, the average member of the union felt that he was a Polish patriot.'[5] Dmowski considered the Socialists' preoccupation with class solidarity objectionable and would have nothing to do with any ideology which implied that the nation was not the most important driving force in history. He secured his first political victory in 1890 when he successfully prevented Warsaw students from organising a sympathy strike in support of students at a Moscow Agricultural Academy. In spite of the Russian students appealing to Polish students for support, Dmowski exploited strong anti-Russian feeling within the Warsaw student community. It was his view that joint action would not be in the Polish students' best interests. While conducting this campaign Dmowski attacked student leaders who were Jewish, implying that they were not truly Polish. Both in the Watchtower and the ZET Dmowski pursued a nationalist agenda, in which anti-Semitism became an important element. While at university he planned demonstrations to celebrate the anniversaries of major historic events to remind Polish youth of the need to fight for independence. On 3 May 1891 Dmowski organised a demonstration in Warsaw to commemorate the Constitution of 3 May 1791. The Russian authorities decided to punish the ringleaders of this illegal demonstration but Dmowski was able to escape them by going on an extended trip abroad.

During this period Dmowski developed his nationalist theories further. He wrote articles for a journal which once again tried to open the debate on Poland's future. His contributions to *Głos* ('The Voice') challenged the idea that Poles could cooperate with the Russian authorities and instead sought to promote the idea of the struggle for independence. Dmowski also had links with an organisation called the Polish League, a broadly-based Nationalist organisation established by two Poles based in Switzerland. His early articles published in *Głos* and his contacts with the Polish League strengthened Dmowski's conviction that the fight for an independent Poland could not be confined to planning for the establishment of a Polish state but that the struggle should be seen as the Polish nation's fight for survival. During his eight-month absence from Poland Dmowski travelled first to Switzerland, where he met Zygmunt Balicki, the founder of the Polish League, and then spent some time in Paris. 'On completion of my studies at the University of Warsaw I went to Paris to further my education and to gain first hand experience of the West,'[6] Dmowski wrote; he always attached importance to personal observation and this trip was the first of many. The critical question which he asked himself during this trip was whether the Western democratic model was the one to which Poles should aspire. These were not idle thoughts. The decision to dedicate himself to politics was forming in his mind.

During this trip Dmowski appears to have decided to abandon plans for a university career and to focus on developing an organisation through which he would be able to pursue his nationalist agenda. This required him to make some personal decisions. In his student years he was considered to be an attractive man and, although lacking funds, could also have counted on developing a promising academic career. In Paris he met and fell in love with a young Polish woman but decided not to pursue her, instead deciding to dedicate himself to politics. This meant that he had to give up plans for marriage and a family, which he knew to be impossible since his activities would bring him into conflict with the authorities. He would always be at risk of arrest and long terms of imprisonment. In years to come it was rumoured that while in exile he fell in love with a young woman who rejected his advances and instead chose to marry Józef Piłsudski. This, many speculated, was the reason why the two men disliked each other so intensely whilst both being dedicated to the fight for a free Poland. In any case it was known that Dmowski attached little importance to marriage as an institution and even less to love, instead claiming to see both as no more than the means of ensuring the survival of the nation, through a careful choice of appropriate partners.

During his journey back to Poland, Dmowski once more stopped in Switzerland and prepared plans with Balicki for a new organisation. Although Dmowski had been warned not to return to Poland he ignored this advice. Remaining in Western Europe was not an option he considered, having in fact formulated a low opinion of Polish student life in Paris. 'I joined an association of Polish youth which took the name Union. Frequent meetings took place usually in an atmosphere of nervous tension as if the fate of Poland depended on what the Union decided. The female members in particular took everything to heart. A contagious atmosphere of mass hysteria was thus generated.'[7] After this, Dmowski decided he would return to political life in Poland, even if it meant he would face the Russian courts and receive a prison sentence. Indeed, no sooner had he arrived at the border of Congress Poland than the Russian authorities arrested him.

As a result he spent five months in the notorious Cytadela prison in Warsaw. When he was released on bail he knew the respite was temporary, and used what he knew would be his last months of freedom to implement the plan agreed with Balicki in Geneva. The Polish League was supposed to bring together Poles from the three Partition areas by reaching out to all sections of society on the basis of a wide-ranging reformist programme. This plan had been too ambitious, however. Dmowski considered that it was time to regroup and to establish a disciplined and focused organisation, replacing the previous loose structure. But before he was able to make further plans the Tsarist authorities announced his sentence. Dmowski was banished from Polish areas under Russian administration for a period of five years, of which three had to be under strict police supervision. In addition he was forbidden to live in any town which had a university. This led to his choosing to stay in a small town near the Baltic city of Riga. But Dmowski had no intention of completing his sentence. In February 1895 he was given permission to go to Warsaw. From there he went south and crossed into the Austrian-controlled part of Poland. By then his political plans for the future had fully formed.

During the period between his return to Congress Poland and his departure into political exile, Dmowski had done his utmost to persuade the leaders of the Polish League to dissolve it. It was to be replaced with a new, distinctly different National League. Moving away from vague schemes for unity, this was an organisation which was to plan for Poles to regain their independence. At that time and while in exile, Dmowski published several articles and pamphlets defining the principles of nationhood, through which he sought to disseminate his ideas and to build an efficient organisation. Up to that time only Socialists had thought in terms of mass parties, ones which cut across vested interests, regions or indeed small communities. Dmowski wanted to build up such an organisation, but one which would unite only Poles on the basis of their shared ethnic origins.

As he fled from Russian Poland areas he implemented a plan which he had formulated earlier. In the first place he settled in Lwów, which was under Austrian control and where police surveillance was relaxed compared to the Russian and German areas. The Austrian authorities had no objection to the use of the Polish language and allowed Polish publications which meant that any materials which were printed in Lwów could be smuggled into areas under Russian and German control where it was impossible to publish in Polish. Lwów was also strategically convenient as a hub from which material could be disseminated as it offered easy access to the Russian-controlled areas. The National League's manifesto was published in a newly-established newspaper. Dmowski's inspirational oratorical style was obvious from the outset. 'We are a nation, a unified, indivisible nation, because we possess a common, collective consciousness, a shared national spirit.' [8] To Dmowski this national spirit would be the driving force of historic change, as he believed it had always been. In that simple formulation he defined the distinctiveness of the newly-emerging movement from Marxist Socialists who spoke of economic factors being the cause of historic changes.

In the following years Dmowski and his collaborators proceeded to build up the National League into an all-Polish conspiratorial organisation. At the same time he decided that the nationalist movement needed to go a step further and to develop a party structure, the aim of which would be to prepare a programme for Poles to attain independence. Thus in May 1897 he announced the formation of a National Democratic Party. In each of the Partition areas there was to be a National Democratic Party united by a common ideology but functioning within the political system of each empire. In Germany and Austria the National Democrats became the largest party representing Polish interests, whereas in the Russian areas it was illegal to form political parties. Access to funding was of critical importance. For that purpose Dmowski once more travelled to France and Switzerland where sympathetic Polish exiles continued to raise funds with the express purpose of assisting the struggle for independence. He also visited the United States and made contact with the Polish communities in Chicago and Cleveland. This did not prove to be a successful trip since the Polish community in the United States, although willing to form associations, did not see the fight for Poland as its main fundraising priority. It is also debatable whether Poles in the United States could have helped Dmowski very much as they were relatively poor, unlike some of the émigré Poles in Western Europe who were prosperous and had links with the Polish and European nobility.

In 1898 Dmowski visited Britain, which he much admired. While in London he stayed in lodgings at 51 Upper Bedford Place near Russell Square and made many visits to the British Museum. His friends later reported that on returning to Lwów, Dmowski expressed admiration for the orderly way in which England appeared to be governed, believing this to be a result of national unity and thus a sign of the strength of the English nation. The fact that the British Empire was at its height would have confirmed his crude Social Darwinist preoccupation with the so-called national spirit and conflict between nations. In years to come Dmowski dreamt of Poland acquiring colonies overseas and visited Brazil where he hoped some territory would be granted to Poland in the future.

The next task was to build a network of couriers who would be able, on a regular basis, to distribute publications throughout Polish areas under Russian control. Any person attempting to enter the Russian Empire with banned publications or caught in possession of materials which were deemed to be seditious risked imprisonment and exile. Dmowski took many risks and even travelled to Warsaw, where if caught he would have faced imprisonment. As the leader of the National League he had to be careful and thus preferred to hold meetings in areas under Austrian control, sometimes in Prague, on other occasions in Budapest where he and his allies continued to plan how to disseminate their propaganda. There was still some risk of being caught, however, as the Austrian and Russian police forces co-operated and were on the lookout for evidence of plots which could threaten the internal stability of the empires. In the long term the National Democrats were successful in their aim of forging a common bond between Poles in the three Partition areas. While the party could have a centralised organisation, Dmowski was able to develop an ideology to which National Democrats in all the Polish areas were committed.

During this time Dmowski continued to develop his idea. The first major work in which he outlined his nationalist theories was *The Thinking of the Modern Pole*.[10] His main preoccupation was the question of who represented the Polish nation. In that he differed from the instigators of the earlier national uprisings, who saw the nobility as having the task of liberating Poland. Dmowski made it clear that he thought the common man was the true carrier of the national spirit. By this he meant the labourers and the peasants. But if this was the case, then how was the National League to reach these people? It indeed was a difficult organisational problem. In Polish areas under Austrian and German control it was possible to establish parties and for them to stand for election to local and national assemblies. But when the National Democratic Party came into existence in 1897 it could not operate in Russian territory. This in turn led to the question of what was to be the party's priority. Was it to be electoral success with a view to securing economic and political advancement for the Polish community or the destruction of the three Empires? Dmowski's answer to this dilemma was unequivocal. Cooperation with the authorities was a betrayal of the Polish national spirit and would only be considered as a step towards the attainment of the ultimate objective of independence for Poland. 'From our standpoint, everything which brings us nearer to that goal, to political independence, is good; everything which diverts us from it is bad – and that is the appropriate measure in matters of national policy.' [11] Thus respect for law was fine for the time being. In reality, all methods would be considered, including the use of force, if they served the national objective. Dmowski was indicating that methods could be flexible, while the ultimate aim was fixed. Violence and aggression were an expression of the superiority and strength of a nation. It was through constant conflicts between nations that the national spirit developed. While admiring the decisiveness of the German state, Dmowski warned that Germany posed the greatest threat to the Polish nation. In line with this reasoning, Russian policies, although brutal, were less purposeful and not at all successful, and because of that were less damaging to the Polish nation. Dmowski believed that in the long term the Russian Empire was the lesser threat.

At the beginning of the 20th century there was evidence of the growth of national self-awareness within the various communities which had previously been part of the Polish-Lithuanian Commonwealth. The Ukrainian, Belorussian and Lithuanian peoples opposed any suggestion that Poland should be reformed within the Commonwealth's old borders. They too started to think of self-determination and independence. Dmowski was uncomfortable with this as he doubted whether these national groups were politically mature enough to establish states of their own. His own reasoning was that although they were ethnically different from the Polish nation they had historically developed side by side with the Poles: 'For the sake of out national future, we face one of two options ... 1) all or some of them , if that is possible, have to become Polish 2) they have to form an independent and strong nation.' [12] His conclusion was that these communities were still incapable of statehood and that they should be absorbed into the Polish nation. This is why he recommended that independent Poland should retain control over the peoples of the Baltic, Belorussia and the Ukraine and that its eastern border should extend from the Baltic to the Black Sea.

'The nation is an absolute reflection of the moral content of the state, and the state is the absolute political form of the nation. A nation might loose its state and it will not cease being a nation, as long as it does not break the moral links with state traditions, if it does not loose the concept of a national state and with that the conscious or unconscious desire to regain its political right to self-determination.'
ROMAN DMOWSKI[13]

The most controversial aspect of Dmowski's theories was his condemnation of the Jews. His ideas on the Jewish question developed over time, but from the outset he saw the Jewish community as a problem distinct from all other ethnic groups. Whereas he was of the opinion that other Slav national groups could be assimilated into the Polish nation, he believed that Jews would weaken the host nation within which they resided. His analysis was based on the conviction that they were a parasitical community deriving its strength from the organisational and economic weakness of the Polish nation. This was a crude pseudo-Darwinian theory applied to Polish history. He justified his deep dislike and distrust of Jews by suggesting that were the Polish nation to be weak, it would be exploited and destroyed by Jews: '… [I]t is the characteristic feature of this race, which never lived a social life as we did, that it had developed and absorbed distinct features, alien to our moral code, and damaging to our life, that any merging with that element would damn us, leading to our young vital elements being replaced with those which will lead to degeneration.' [14] Dmowski drew attention to the supposed low birth rate among ethnic Poles and the alleged high birth rate in Jewish communities. Thus he advised that the only way to counteract this threat was to become a strong nation and to expel the foreign body from its midst.

During the second half of the 19th century Polish-Jewish relations had been exacerbated by Russian discriminatory policies. Since 1791 Jews in the Russian Empire could only live in a designated area, the so-called Pale of Settlement. This area extended across the Baltic coast, Belorussia, Ukraine and Eastern Poland. The borders were not fixed and changed according to the whim of the regime. Poles within Russian areas resented this policy as it increased the concentration of Jewish people in Polish territory. By law Jews were obliged to live in urban areas, usually in abject poverty. In most cases they lived by small-scale production and retailing which increased tension between Polish and Jewish craftsmen. The distinctiveness of these communities attracted attention and prejudice in equal measure.

Dmowski's main aim was to see the reconstruction of a Polish state. He emphatically disagreed with Polish leaders who believed that Poles should be reconciled to the loss of independence. Therefore all his political plans and those of the National Democrats were focused on exploiting every opportunity to secure independence. Electoral successes in the German and Austrian assemblies were important indicators of the movement's popular appeal, but still did not offer an opportunity for Poles to reclaim their independence. Dmowski, as a subject of the Russian Empire, could not play a direct role in the political life of the Polish areas incorporated in Germany and Austria. Nevertheless, he was keenly aware of the National Democrats' successes in elections to the national assemblies in each of the Partition areas. In 1903 three National Democrats won seats to the German assembly. During the elections to the first Russian Duma which took place in 1906 eight National Democrats were returned. In 1907 17 National Democrats represented the Polish National group in the Vienna assembly. His own concern, however, was that the party should focus on mobilisation of the Polish community for the purpose of securing independence. This explains why, in common with Polish national leaders of all political persuasions, Dmowski carefully studied the international situation to see whether the consensus between the Russian, Austrian and German empires was as strong as it had been when the Polish-Lithuanian Commonwealth was partitioned. In 1903 it looked as if an international crisis was likely to engulf the Russian Empire when it was confronted by the growth of Japanese power in the Far East. The leaders of the National Democratic movement in Poland made contact with leaders of other national groups in the Russian Empire, hoping to make joint preparations for the moment when, as they assumed, the war would cause the Russian Empire to implode and thus allow them to claim independence. The most promising of these talks were with the Finns, but at this stage it was too early to do anything other than to plan for the future. Dmowski was opposed to a national uprising, fearing that were it to take place prematurely the Poles would once more suffer bloody reprisals from Russian troops.

When war between Russia and Japan broke out on 8 February 1904 Dmowski was ready. On the basis that 'the enemy of your enemy is your friend', he believed that Japan would be interested in helping the Poles destabilise the Russian Empire. He immediately set out for Tokyo. The purpose of his visit appears to have been twofold, although it remains unclear which was the most important objective: to secure Japanese support for Polish aspirations or to prevent a fellow Pole, the leader of the Polish Socialist party Józef Piłsudski, whom he knew to be making the same journey, from persuading the Japanese to support his own party's objectives. Ideological and personal issues divided the two men, and Dmowski was determined to ensure that any assistance the Japanese rendered the Poles would not contribute to the establishment of an independent Poland governed by a Socialist party.

Dmowski and Piłsudski met in Japan, which caused both men embarrassment. As well as asking the Japanese General Staff if they could form a legion to fight Russia from amongst Polish prisoners of war, Piłsudski also wanted their support for an armed uprising in Poland, which he suggested would cause the Russians considerable military difficulties. Dmowski took a different line and asked the Japanese not to finance uprisings in Poland, reasoning that the Russians would then keep units in Polish territory in anticipation of trouble. Both men made the intriguing connection between the Far Eastern conflict and the Polish question, but in the end the Japanese were unwilling to devote resources to what they saw as a side-show.

Nevertheless the Japanese military victory over Russia resulted in positive developments, which Dmowski was able to exploit. The defeat of the Russian army and navy as well as economic problems led to strikes in all major industrial towns in the European parts of Russia and in the Polish territories. Reluctantly Tsar Nicholas II was persuaded to make concessions of which the convening of an elected assembly, the Duma, was the most important. This opened up new opportunities to fight the Polish cause by means of parliamentary politics. Dmowski had been horrified by the strikes and fighting which affected Warsaw and the industrial town of Łódź in 1905. He accused the Socialists of having stirred up fratricidal conflicts. On hearing of the Tsar's decision to allow for the formation of an elected assembly, Dmowski saw this as an opportunity for Poles to secure first autonomy within the Empire and then independence. He had by then become the leading spokesman of the National Democratic movement and his authority was immense. He was not able to stand for the first elections to the Duma but in 1907 he became a deputy for Warsaw. In view of the growing Russian-German conflict he had come to believe that the Russian Empire would be willing to make concessions to the Poles.[15] As before, Dmowski's motives were complex. It has been suggested that he was shaken by the realisation that Poles would succumb to revolutionary ideas and that, in spite of his hope that workers would remain steadfastly committed to the national cause, that they could, and indeed during the revolutionary months of 1905 and 1906 did, take to the streets hoping to establish a Socialist state. This drove him on to push the National Democratic agenda more forcefully than previously and to take his seat in the Duma.

The reality of the Russian concessions proved to be a bitter blow to Dmowski's hopes that Poles could negotiate autonomy within the Empire. As soon as order was re-established Tsar Nicholas reneged on many of the concessions and changed the electoral law, by increasing the representation of the wealthy townspeople and the landowners in the Duma, as he believed that these groups would be more likely to support the regime. The autocratic system remained in place with only minor changes and with that the Russian regime showed its determination to prevent the Poles from gaining independence.

The period between 1907, when Dmowski was seen to co-operate with the hated Russians, and the outbreak of the war in 1914 was a difficult time for him. He valiantly maintained his conviction that Russia would change its policy on the Polish question, though there was no evidence to substantiate this. The only way out of the stalemate was the hope of a crisis which would force the Russian regime to reconsider its position. Thus Dmowski became increasingly preoccupied with the possibility of war breaking out. By 1908, with Austria-Hungary's occupation of Bosnia and Hercegovina, an air of foreboding hung over Europe. There was general anticipation that some minor incident would lead to a breakdown in the European consensus, as a result of which Germany, allied to Austria-Hungary, would be at war with Russia.

# 3
# The First World War

The outbreak of a Europe-wide conflict in 1914, the ferocity and scale of which created new opportunities which the Poles were quick to exploit, had been anticipated since the turn of the century. The united front of Austria, Germany and Russia, which had dominated Eastern and Central Europe during the preceding century and had ensured that the various subjugated national groups did not succeed in their bids for independence, came to an end. The inevitable consequence of the deterioration of relations between the three empires was the likelihood of Poland emerging as an independent state. In 1914 it was impossible to predict what the borders of the new state would be, nor the degree of independence it would be able to enjoy. Initially Polish leaders hoped for a Poland with some degree of autonomy within one of the empires.

The war was sparked by an incident which, though shocking, was not in itself the cause of the European war. On 28 July 1914 a Serbian terrorist assassinated Archduke Franz Ferdinand, the heir to the Austro-Hungarian throne, and his wife in Sarajevo. This set in motion a course of events which ultimately resulted in Russia, in alliance with France and Great

**Europe 1914**

Petrograd (St Petersburg)

Riga

Moscow

Vilna

Königsberg

**RUSSIAN EMPIRE**

Warsaw     Brest-Litovsk

Kiev

apest     Odessa

**ROMANIA**
Bucharest     *Black Sea*

grade

SERBIA     **BULGARIA**
Sofia

Constantinople

**GREECE**     **OTTOMAN EMPIRE**

Athens

Britain, facing a hostile Germany allied to Austria-Hungary. While in the West the war bogged down in a continuous line of trenches across French and Belgian territory, in the East the fighting raged over widely extended areas. In North-Eastern Europe most of the fighting initially took place in Polish territories. Casualty rates were high as were the numbers of prisoners taken. Polish men, depending on the area where they lived, were conscripted into either the Austrian, Russian or German armies. They were likewise captured by the enemy, becoming prisoners of war of empires which at the same time were conscripting their own Polish subjects. The situation was extremely confused, no doubt made much more complex by the dawning realisation that as the war continued, there was a need to try and defuse internal tensions. Thus demands made by national groups for concessions became a factor both in attempts to secure the population's support for a prolonged war and in efforts to undermine the enemy's internal stability. The Poles, like other nationalities, were quick to exploit these factors by presenting demands for a greater degree of independence. Thus while the Austrian government tried to maintain the multinational structure of its empire, at the same time it did everything possible to undermine the cohesiveness of the Russian empire. The Russians likewise took every opportunity to encourage the Slavic population of the Habsburg Empire to rebel.

In the East the offensive was initially taken by the Russians, who on 17 August 1914 attacked the German army in East Prussia. In spite of initial successes the Russians were forced back and as a result of two major defeats, at Tannenberg then at Masurian Lakes, were driven out of East Prussia. In the South, however, the Austrian offensive against the Russian army was disastrous. An early thrust towards Russian-held

Warsaw failed and by the end of August Austria had abandoned Galicia and the Russian army had the initiative. To the German High Command the Eastern Front was of great importance. It was therefore decided to give it priority over the Western Front and to move troops from that front to the east in order to defeat the Russians. In May efforts were co-ordinated but with the Germans firmly in control. On 5 August 1915 Warsaw was occupied by the Germans and the Austrians then captured Lublin. The Russian army gave way and the Germans swept East. By 25 August, when the German army reached Brest-Litovsk, the Eastern Front had collapsed. Polish territory previously held by the Russians, as well as the Baltic coast, was in German hands and since the Russians were unable to launch a counter-offensive all Polish territory remained under joint German-Austrian control until the end of the war.

During the fighting Polish territory had been devastated. All three powers made full use of Polish manpower and resources. Pillaging and exploitation led to the destruction of forests, buildings and industry. But worse was to follow. As Germany and Austria assumed control over Polish areas so the issue of post-war arrangements was addressed by the army commanders. The Germans dominated all decision-making, ignoring Austrian interests in Polish territories. Occupied areas remained firmly under military administration. General Erich von Ludendorff, the architect of the military victory against the Russians, was appointed Quartermaster-General (in effect deputy Chief of the General Staff) to Field Marshal Hindenburg. Their policy was to assume absolute control of civilian affairs in order to fully mobilise resources for the war effort. This had a terrible impact on Polish territories as food, stores and all industrial production were taken by the

German army. But the army's planning extended beyond how to control occupied Poland during the war. Plans were made for how the Eastern areas could be retained either under direct or indirect German control after the war. The aim was to ensure that the industrialised areas, previously under Russian control, would not compete with German industry.

The war led to population movements on a scale unprecedented in the history of Eastern Europe. In Polish territories where major battles had taken place, thousands of people fled in advance of the armies. The Russian policy of removing vital industries into the interior, taking all the workers with them, resulted in the displacement of many Poles deep into Russia.

Although Germany and Austria were firmly in control of all Polish territory, the war in the West was inconclusive and that meant that neither side was willing to address the Polish question in the long term. Instead the need to secure civilian support for the war effort came to dominate all discussions. This gave the leaders of national groups an opportunity to try and start the debate on what might happen after the war. From the outset Polish leaders sought to ascertain whether the belligerent powers could be persuaded to make promises concerning the future of Poland. In order to gain influence they asked for the establishment of Polish volunteer military units. The thinking behind these requests was twofold. Firstly, a visible Polish contribution to the war effort would bolster the Poles' sense of national pride and purpose, while secondly Polish national leaders calculated that in view of the shortage of manpower, each of the belligerents would appreciate the Polish contribution and would reward them with assurances of independence after the war. The Polish leaders were playing a dangerous game, however, as they had no way of knowing which side was likely to win the war and whether promises made during it would actually be respected.

On 14 August 1914, in an effort to retain the support of his Polish subjects during the war, Grand Duke Nicholas of Russia made a Proclamation to the Poles: '... The soul of Poland is not dead. It has lived with the hope that the hour of resurrection of the Polish nation and of its fraternal reconciliation with Great Russia will come.'[1] The reality was disappointing. This dramatic reference to the resurrection of the Polish nation were not accompanied by any assurance that Russia would allow the Poles the right to self-determination. The Polish deputies in the Duma agonised over the Proclamation, trying to find some hope for the future. They found none and even Dmowski, who still reasoned that a strong Germany was the greatest natural enemy of an independent Poland, became despondent. Reluctantly, however, in December 1914 the Russian army allowed the formation of the Polish-manned Puławski Legion. Still, the Polish leaders remained uneasy.

> '... The soul of Poland is not dead. It has lived with the hope that the hour of resurrection of the Polish nation and of its fraternal reconciliation with Great Russia will come.'
> **GRAND DUKE NICHOLAS OF RUSSIA, 14 AUGUST 1914**

Of all the Partition powers, Austria had been the most willing to grant the Poles wide autonomy within their Empire. Thus, initially many Poles looked to Austria in the hope that, were it to be successful in occupying Polish areas under Russian control, it would agree to resurrect the Polish Kingdom within the framework of the Austro-Hungarian Empire. In 1908 Piłsudski moved to Austrian-ruled Galicia. At that time the Socialist movement was split over the question of how to respond to the growing international tension caused by the Austrian annexation of Bosnia and Herce-govina. Some thought that Poland should ally itself with Russia, while the faction led by Piłsudski decided that Austria was most likely to win in any future conflict and that it would be a good idea to militarily prepare for this possibility. In 1910 Austria introduced legislation allowing for the formation of riflemens' associations. Piłsudski was given permission to raise two such units from the Polish population, which he hoped would become the backbone of a future Polish army.[2]

When war broke out the Austrians allowed him to lead his units into Russian-controlled Poland. Piłsudski planned to proceed to Warsaw which he believed he could capture, but the local population did not come to his support and he had to withdraw.

With the German military victories came the realisa-tion that the German High Command and not the Austri-ans would have the final say on the Polish question. Austria gave way to Germany there, focusing on the Adriatic and Romania, areas which were of greater strategic importance to the Habsburgs. On 5 November 1916 the German and Austrian Emperors jointly issued a proclamation. Once more florid language hid paucity of content: '... Overwhelmed by steadfast faithfulness in the ultimate victory of their arms, and guided by the wish that the Polish lands wrenched from Russian domination by heavy sacrifices of our gallant armies be led to a happy future ... [we] decided to form from these lands an autonomous State with a hereditary monarch and a constitutional regime. A more precise delimination of its frontiers is reserved.'[3] In order give substance to this vague assurance the Germans put together a Provisional Council of State of the Kingdom of Poland to which they appointed a number of obliging Poles. Its precise role was undecided,

## JÓZEF PIŁSUDSKI (1867–1935)

Józef Piłsudski's early years bore some similarities to those of Paderewski. Born in Lithuania, an area which had been part of the Polish-Lithuanian Commonwealth, he was brought up in a deeply patriotic household. During his studies he came into contact with Russian revolutionaries and as a result became a Socialist. As penalty for involvement in student politics, the Tsarist authorities sentenced him to five years' internal exile in 1887. When he returned he became a leading light in the Polish Socialist Party, representing the faction which considered that the fight for independent Poland was as important as the fight for Socialism. The National Democrats distrusted the Socialists, fearing that they would lead Polish workers into reckless conflict with the Tsarist authorities. In 1908 Piłsudski concluded that even if a revolution took place in Russia Poland would not secure independence. He thus decided to investigate the possibility of whether the Austrian authorities would allow him to form a Polish paramilitary organisation. Since Austria increasingly assumed that a conflict with Russia was inevitable, they encouraged Piłsudski. By then he had moved away from his Socialist roots. When war broke out, Piłsudski was committed to the Central Powers in the belief that they would win and ultimately agree to Polish independence. In 1917, however, he fell out with the German military authorities when they tried to use Polish military units without giving any assurances on Polish independence. When Germany was defeated, Piłsudski played a critical role in the transfer of power to the newly-established Polish authority. His reputation as military commander was such that in November 1918 he was given control of the new Polish army. Under his leadership Poland's eastern borders were defined through a series of conflicts with the Ukrainians, Belorussians and Lithuanians and finally also in the Russian war of 1920. During the years that followed Piłsudski assiduously cultivated his legend as a political leader which enabled him to lead a military coup in May 1926 when the majority of political parties supported him in preventing the National Democrats from taking power. In reality Piłsudski had little time for democracy and after 1926 established a regime based on the army. In 1934 he and his coterie introduced a new constitution which reduced the power of the legislature in favour of the executive. When he died on 12 May 1935 he was succeeded by a group of military leaders whose government came to be known as the 'Rule of the Colonels'.

thus leading to further frustration among the Polish leaders. In reality, the German and Austrian armies, increasingly short of manpower, hoped to extend recruitment into recently-occupied Polish areas.[4] But the Poles, only too aware of the wanton destruction and exploitation of resources they had suffered, distrusted German and Austrian proclamations and held back from volunteering. Nor was the German High Command happy to see its authority in occupied Polish areas challenged by decisions made in Berlin and Vienna, where already discussions were taking place on the granting of some autonomy to the Poles after the war. The conflict came to a head at the beginning of July 1917 when Piłsudski objected to the incorporation of the Polish Legions into the German army. He was promptly arrested and held in the notorious Magdeburg military prison.[5]

The German and Austrian declaration had an impact on the other belligerent states. The first to respond was Russia. Reluctant to go beyond what had already been promised at the beginning of the war, the Russian Prime Minister merely stated that Polish areas under Russian control would be united, although Poland would remain part of the Russian Empire. Although the Russians were willing to continue recruitment into the Puławski Legion, this was done without conviction, thus alienating even those loyalists who would have wanted post-war Poland to remain allied to its powerful Slav neighbour.

In France and Britain various Polish emissaries attempted to persuade the governments to declare publicly that the creation of an independent Poland was one of their war aims. In their efforts to influence the Western Allies, the self-appointed Polish representatives such as Paderewski and Dmowski had to battle with the stark fact that Poland's fate was not of critical importance to either government. On the contrary, were the two governments to make premature promises to the Poles, this could have unleashed a veritable 'bidding war' with the other national minorities in the Austro-Hungarian, Russian and Ottoman Empires making their own claims for independence. As long as there was a chance that Austria-Hungary could be persuaded to make a separate peace, the Entente Powers remained silent on the question of national self-determination for the Empire's minorities. Mindful of the need to maintain an Eastern Front, neither France nor Britain wanted to embarrass Russia by making an announcement which could be interpreted as a post-war condition. The rights of national groups within the Russian Empire was too thorny an issue to tackle at a time when Russia was a valued ally. This explains why, in spite of extensive lobbying, the Polish leaders were only able to affect British and French thinking on the Polish question when it became clear that Austria would not abandon Germany and when the United States made commitments which went beyond what Britain and France had decided. But until that happened the Allies merely confined themselves to pious pronouncements. In the meantime, the need for manpower introduced a degree of flexibility in responses to Polish lobbying. The French were only too willing to accept an offer from Polish émigrés to form a Polish Legion which would fight alongside the French army, but that did not in itself change its policies towards Poland.

> **'The Allied nations are conscious that they are fighting not for selfish interests but, above all, to safeguard the independence of peoples, right and humanity.'**
> **ALLIED POWERS' NOTE TO PRESIDENT WILSON, 18 DECEMBER 1916[6]**

The outbreak of the war had electrified the Polish community abroad. At the time of the crisis caused by the assassination in Sarajevo, Paderewski was at home in Switzerland. On 31 July 1914 he had planned a large party to celebrate his name day, more of an occasion than a birthday in the Polish community. As it happened, Dmowski was visiting him. Paderewski recalled: *There was a peculiar atmosphere among all the guests. Every one, without knowing exactly why, was under the impression that something was about to happen – that something must happen. It affected the whole gathering and threw a strange kind of gloom over the gaiety at supper.*[7] The news of the declaration of war came during that evening. Dmowski received a telegram, as a result of which he immediately left for Warsaw, from where he hastened to Petrograd. Paderewski's French and Swiss guests dispersed to change into military uniforms. Their host was shocked next morning to see all the men in uniform. In his memoirs he mentions that they had in arrived at his house carrying *little valises* in which they evidently had their uniforms.[8] The unmistakable signs of general mobilisation for a European war were there for all to see. His personal circumstances changed too. Funds which foreigners had earlier deposited in Swiss banks were frozen, leaving destitute those who only a few days before had enjoyed affluent lifestyles. In Paderewski's case an exception was made and he was allowed to draw a small daily allowance. He nevertheless concentrated immediately on securing support for Poland, initially in the form of assistance for Polish refugees.

During the first year of war the Polish communities in exile in Switzerland and in France coordinated their activities and devised a three-pronged strategy. Dmowski and the National Democrats still thought that Polish interests would be best served by close collaboration with Russia, so Dmowski returned to Petrograd where he hoped to defend the Polish cause in the Duma. In areas of Congress Poland the aim was to bring together influential personalities who would pool their abilities and resources to devise a plan for a post-war Poland. In West European capitals, firstly relief organisations and secondly political pressure groups were to be formed to secure funds and to gain access to influential persons.

In spite of this apparent consensus Paderewski and the writer Henryk Sienkiewicz found themselves at loggerheads with a number of other famous Polish exiles, most notably the author Joseph Conrad, as to how to proceed. They quickly became aware that France could not be persuaded to publicly declare its support for any plans for the creation of an independent Poland at the end of the war. That would have offended the Russians who would have seen such talk as an attempt to sanction the break-up of their Empire. France's desperate military situation and the need for Russia to maintain the Eastern Front against Germany and Austria meant that all French politicians were extremely cautious about how to approach the Polish question. Paderewski understood this predicament and was willing to play for time, focusing initially on helping Polish refugees. In an attempt to pacify the French, he went along with suggestions that the Russian ambassadors in Switzerland and France should be invited to act as patrons of the Polish Victims Relief Fund. When some Poles objected to this, Paderewski tried to remove himself from the infighting. In March 1915 he went to London where he used his old social contacts to raise funds. *I was greeted very warmly but with the same hesitation as in France. Everyone, from Asquith to Cardinal Bourne, told me that they will join the Relief Committee on the condition that the Russian*

*Ambassador will also be a member. Britain was allied, so they could do nothing that would lead to misunderstandings or conflicts with the Russians.*[9] The list of those who were persuaded to act as honorary patrons to the fund reads like a *Who's Who* of the period, and included Asquith, Lloyd George, Lord Rosebery, Lord Grey, Lord Northcliffe, Rudyard Kipling and the opera singer Nellie Melba. The Rothschild family's support was secured to counteract accusations of anti-Semitism within Paderewski's organisation.

In April 1915 Paderewski made the momentous decision to go to the United States. Although the United States was still neutral, Paderewski was personally convinced that this would not last, although at this stage there was there still no public indication that the United States would become involved in the European war.[10] On the contrary, strong pressure from the German-speaking community and the well-organised Irish lobby to stay out of the war dominated the media. Paderewski nevertheless believed that the United States, as the most powerful state in the world, would have a decisive say after the war and was optimistic regarding its support. *I came to the United States with the aim of stimulating interest and sympathy for my country. I calculated that the war would last a long time and that the United States would be morally compelled to take part in it.*[11] He also earlier developed the idea that the Poles should preside over the creation of a United States of Poland, which would embrace the territories of the old Polish-Lithuanian Commonwealth, modelled on the American constitution.

In the United States Paderewski set out to fully exploit his standing as a famous musician to win support for the Polish cause. He toured the United States coast to coast giving short lectures on Poland's history and current event.

His fundraising efforts were very successful and thousands of dollars were raised for the Relief Fund. But Paderewski also learned that he could make direct appeals for the United States to support Poland's restoration to the map of Europe. He had to be diplomatic and that he was fully prepared to do. He used his charm, his charisma and intellect to schmooze all sections of American society, travelling from small hamlets to large industrial towns. For his cause to succeed he needed the full support of the Polish community, which until then had shown little natural unity. In putting the Polish issue at the top of the United States' agenda, he had to contend with the fact that the majority of Polish-Americans held unskilled jobs and had little political influence. Paderewski was determined that they should not be ashamed of being Polish; they were not to define themselves as the proverbial 'Polacks' but as Poles with a proud history and a great cultural heritage.

> 'I came to the United States with the aim of stimulating interest and sympathy for my country. I calculated that the war would last a long time and that the United States would be morally compelled to take part in it.'
>
> **IGNACY PADEREWSKI**

While Paderewski's efforts were successful in every respect, his campaign coincided with a growing awareness that the United States should take a closer interest in what was happening in Europe. The Wilson administration was trying to understand what the implications of the fast-developing events in Europe were and there was a need for more information. In November 1916 Paderewski, through one of his old social contacts, met Colonel Edward House, one of Wilson's closest advisers. Having persuaded House that he was a very influential person in European politics, Paderewski then

## PRESIDENT WILSON'S FOURTEEN POINTS, 8 JANUARY 1918

The program of the world's peace, therefore, is our program; and that program, the only possible program, as we see it, is this:

I. Open covenants of peace, openly arrived at, after which there shall be no private international understandings of any kind but diplomacy shall proceed always frankly and in the public view.

II. Absolute freedom of navigation upon the seas, outside territorial waters, alike in peace and in war, except as the seas may be closed in whole or in part by international action for the enforcement of international covenants.

III. The removal, so far as possible, of all economic barriers and the establishment of an equality of trade conditions among all the nations consenting to the peace and associating themselves for its maintenance.

IV. Adequate guarantees given and taken that national armaments will be reduced to the lowest point consistent with domestic safety.

V. A free, open-minded, and absolutely impartial adjustment of all colonial claims, based upon a strict observance of the principle that in determining all such questions of sovereignty the interests of the populations concerned must have equal weight with the equitable claims of the government whose title is to be determined.

VI. The evacuation of all Russian territory and such a settlement of all questions affecting Russia as will secure the best and freest cooperation of the other nations of the world in obtaining for her an unhampered and unembarrassed opportunity for the independent determination of her own political development and national policy and assure her of a sincere welcome into the society of free nations under institutions of her own choosing; and, more than a welcome, assistance also of every kind that she may need and may herself desire. The treatment accorded Russia by her sister nations in the months to come will be the acid test of their good will, of their comprehension of her needs as distinguished from their own interests, and of their intelligent and unselfish sympathy.

VII. Belgium, the whole world will agree, must be evacuated and restored, without any attempt to limit the sovereignty which she enjoys in common with all other free nations. No other single act will serve as this will serve to restore confidence among the nations in the laws which they have themselves set and determined for the government of their relations with one another. Without this healing act the whole structure and validity of international law is forever impaired.

VIII. All French territory should be freed and the invaded portions restored, and the wrong done to France by Prussia in 1871 in the matter of Alsace-Lorraine, which has unsettled the peace of the world for nearly fifty years, should be righted, in order that peace may once more be made secure in the interest of all.

IX. A readjustment of the frontiers of Italy should be effected along clearly recognizable lines of nationality.

X. The peoples of Austria-Hungary, whose place among the nations we wish to see safeguarded and assured, should be accorded the freest opportunity to autonomous development.

XI. Rumania, Serbia, and Montenegro should be evacuated; occupied territories restored; Serbia accorded free and secure access to the sea; and the relations of the several Balkan states to one another determined by friendly counsel along historically established lines of allegiance and nationality; and international guarantees of the political and economic independence and territorial integrity of the several Balkan states should be entered into.

XII. The Turkish portion of the present Ottoman Empire should be assured a secure sovereignty, but the other nationalities which are now under Turkish rule should be assured an undoubted security of life and an absolutely unmolested opportunity of autonomous development, and the Dardanelles should be permanently opened as a free passage to the ships and commerce of all nations under international guarantees.

XIII. An independent Polish state should be erected which should include the territories inhabited by indisputably Polish populations, which should be assured a free and secure access to the sea, and whose political and economic independence and territorial integrity should be guaranteed by international covenant.

XIV. A general association of nations must be formed under specific covenants for the purpose of affording mutual guarantees of political independence and territorial integrity to great and small states alike.

secured an invitation to the White House. Wilson was by then ready to listen to an analysis of the consequences of the likely break-up of the old European empires. The President and his wife were charmed by the romantic pianist. On 6 November, at the end of their first meeting, Wilson made a personal declaration to Paderewski of his support: 'My dear Paderewski, I can tell you that Poland will be resurrected and will exist again.' [12]

In January 1917, when the Wilson administration discussed the possible outcome of the war, Paderewski was asked to submit a memorandum on the Polish question to the President. This he did at lightning speed. The presidential advisers who had read it stated that it was a poetic essay, one which captured the soul and spirit of the Polish nation while at the same time demanding extensive territory.[13] The document dated 11 November 1916 is credited with swaying the President in favour of the Polish case. This is doubtful, but to the end of his life Paderewski believed this to have been so. On 22 January 1917 President Wilson solemnly declared to the Senate: 'Any peace which did not recognise and accept the principle that governments derive their power from the consent of the governed neither could nor should be lasting … I believe that statesmen everywhere are agreed on the question that there should be a united, free and independent Poland'.[14] Poland's future looked assured if the European Allies followed the Presidential declaration with similar ones of their own. On 6 April 1917 the United States declared war on Germany and Austria. Nevertheless, the strongest guarantee that Poland would be restored came in the thirteenth of Wilson's famous Fourteen Points.

Paderewski had staked everything on gaining the support of the United States and in that he appeared to have been right even before President Wilson decided to declare war. Dmowski, as noted earlier, had followed a different policy. When the war broke out he had believed that Russia would win and that Poles should collaborate with the Russians in the hope of achieving autonomy within the Empire, rather than heed calls for a national uprising which the Russians would suppress violently. By November 1915, however, Dmowski realised that the Russians were not going to grant the Poles their long-cherished independence. Still maintaining that Germany was Poland's main enemy, he left Petrograd to lobby the British and French governments in the hope that in due course they would force the Russians to make a commitment on the Polish question. He arrived in Switzerland in December, and travelled on to London and Paris. He based himself in London, and made some headway.[15] Cambridge University awarded him an honorary degree, and he met some of the foremost writers of the time, such as Hilaire Belloc and G K Chesterton. A number of Foreign Office advisers on Central Europe sought his views and Dmowski submitted extensive memoranda to the Foreign Office, but his influence on actual decision-making was minimal. Although Dmowski was persistent in his efforts to persuade the British government of the need to support the Polish cause, the Foreign Office was divided. In 1916 it debated the Polish case as part of a review of war aims. The conclusion was that Britain should support the reconstruction of Poland within ethnic boundaries, linked to the Russian Empire.[16] This view had not changed by the end of the war, but unfortunately for the Polish cause the Foreign Office view of Dmowski had hardened against him. Initially there were a number of officials who supported him and his vision of a Poland as a barrier against Germany, among them John Duncan Gregory, a junior clerk, and Sir Eric Drummond, private secretary to the Secretary of State for Foreign Affairs. But even they were repulsed by Dmowski's anti-Semitism. Lord Robert Cecil, the Parliamentary Under-secretary of State and Arthur Balfour, who in December 1916 became Foreign Secretary, were hostile to Dmowski's ideology and to his vision of a Poland which was to incorporate non-Polish nationals.[17] Dmowski himself blamed the Jewish Lewis Namier, an adviser to the Foreign Office whose pronounced dislike of his vision for Poland was well known, for having supposedly determined British policy.

While London was his base, Dmowski moved between Paris and Switzerland, the two places where the influential émigré community was active in keeping the Polish issue on the international agenda. Dmowski's reputation was such that he was able to secure the support of those within that community who believed that the Polish cause would be best served through co-operation with the Entente Powers. This did not happen without a struggle but by 1917 Dmowski had established his authority. To reinforce Polish influence on British and French plans, Dmowski and his collaborators focused on first obtaining French permission for the creation of a Polish army in the West. Whereas initially France and Britain were still reluctant to make clear commitments, the Russian Revolution changed everything. On 15 August 1917 a Polish National Committee (KNP) was formed in Lausanne to represent the Polish case to the Entente Powers. By then the French government had agreed to the formation of a Polish army for which the KNP assumed responsibility. On 20 September the French government accepted the KNP as representing Polish interests. Britain did likewise on 15 October. Italy and the United States followed with statements that they recognised the authority of the KNP on 30 October. The scene looked set for the Dmowski-led KNP to soon become a provisional government. In years to come Dmowski was to express regret that this did not happen. 'If only we had been able to act as the representatives of the Polish nation … if only we would have been able to speak and make undertakings on behalf of all Poland, without provoking noisy protests from our enemies, from the outset the Polish case would have been presented differently and it would have been resolved differently.' [18] Dmowski was speaking of his enemies within the Polish community in exile but also of those Polish leaders, most notably Piłsudski, who had in the meantime made the decision to go along with German plans in Polish areas under the occupation of the Central Powers.

> 'We … started as allies of the Russian oppressors of Poland, with the Polish soldiers of Silesia and Galicia fighting against us.'
> **GEORGES CLEMENCEAU[19]**

The outbreak of the revolution in Russia in February 1917 and the collapse of the Eastern Front injected a sense of urgency into debates on war aims. Britain and France had to consider how they would cope with a German onslaught on the Western Front. In those circumstances anything which would weaken the German war effort had to be considered, and therefore there was a new-found willingness to make open declarations regarding Poland. The October Revolution and the news of the opening of the German-Russian peace talks added a new element to the fast-evolving situation. The Entente Powers' commitment to the restoration of Poland increased with the publication of President Wilson's Fourteen Points. The signing of the Treaty of Brest-Litovsk between Germany and the Bolshevik government in January 1918 removed any further apprehension. The main difference between President Wilson's statement of US war aims and the

French and British view was that the latter would have pre-ferred to leave discussion of all issues relating to Central and Eastern Europe until after the war. This meant that while they in principle agreed to the restoration of Poland, they were still not certain of its future borders and the way in which Poland would emerge. Brest-Litovsk removed France's last apprehen-sions, however, as it underlined the need for plans to weaken Germany. Thus on 3 June 1918 Britain and France declared that the restoration of a free Poland with access to the sea was one of their war aims. The military victory against the Central Powers was not completed until November 1918, but the diplomatic struggle for an independent Poland had been won.

12 May 1926 Józef Piłsudski and five loyal generals crossing the Poniatowski bridge from the district of Praga to the capital. The Regiment of Light Cavalry had secured the bridge. Troops loyal to Poniatowski were grouped in the suburb of Rembertow on the right bank of the Wisła. The length of the shadows suggests that this photo was taken in the afternoon when Piłsudski made his second crossing to meet President Wojciechowski. During the afternoon the president refused to dismiss the Prime Minister Witos, which led to three days of fighting between troops loyal to Piłsudski and those who remained steadfast in supporting the government. 215 soldier and 164 civilians died as a result of the street fighting.

## II

# The Paris Peace Conference

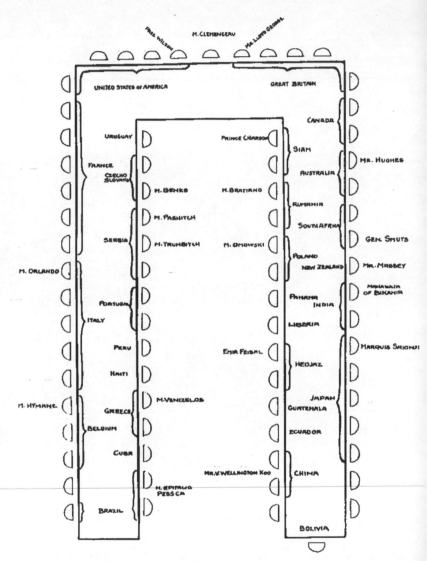

Sketch of the seating plan at the Paris Peace Conference.

# 4

## The Emergence of Independent Poland

Paderewski and Dmowski were both convinced that while Poland's independence had been won on the diplomatic front, Britain and France, together with the United States, would still have a major say in what happened after the war. To that end, both leaders focused on transforming what had been a dream of independence on the part of a minor East European nation into no less than a test of international political morality. During 1918 it looked as if they had succeeded in placing the Polish issue high on the post-war agenda. Even before the Entente's victory over the Central Powers was assured they had made a commitment to the Polish cause. At the beginning of 1918, therefore, the KNP began to prepare in earnest submissions on the future borders of Poland.[1]

Although it appeared that everything would be decided at the negotiating table, throughout the last year of the war the struggle for independent Poland was fought on several fronts. Dmowski was elected to act as chairman of the KNP and had its full confidence. However, interestingly, his authority within the National Democratic Party was not so secure;

many at home felt that he had focused all his efforts on international affairs and had neglected to build up a domestic power base.[2] But the fact was that the diplomatic battle took place in London and in Paris, and it was there that the KNP tried to make the most of the Entente Powers' desire to plan for a post-war European settlement. In the United States Paderewski conducted a campaign to unite the Polish community so that it could more effectively put pressure on Congress to put the Polish question high on the list of war aims. Although the Polish lobby in France had had to tread carefully in the early years of the war, by 1917 its leaders, galvanised by Paderewski's diplomatic efforts, felt bold enough to transform themselves into a political lobby group with the explicit aim of becoming a provisional government. The establishment of the KNP on 15 August 1917 marked a break from simple relief work. Henceforth its aim was to secure recognition of the government of the future Polish state. Its members set out to increase public awareness of the Polish case by sending memoranda to the British Foreign Office and to the French Ministry for Foreign Affairs, and by raising a Polish army in France to fight alongside the Entente. In the Polish areas under German and Austrian control, Piłsudski had offered military support in return for a commitment to the creation of an independent state. While Paderewski and Dmowski communicated with each other and coordinated their campaigns, they both neglected to address the possibility of Piłsudski assuming control over events in Poland itself. This he did with the near-complete support of all the political parties there.[3]

Dmowski and Paderewski had moved along similar lines. Both had hoped to see the establishment of some form of political organisation in the West which could in due course become a provisional government. They both also knew that their demands would be strengthened by the active participation of Polish forces in the war. Thus separately, one in the United States and the other in France pursued similar tactics. Dmowski knew that the KNP was too narrowly-based to claim to be truly representative and that neither the Socialist Party nor the Peasant Alliance, which had a considerable following within the Polish community, would accept the KNP's claim to be acting as a provisional government unless it was reorganised to include them. The KNP leaders were National Democrats, notably Dmowski, Maurycy Zamoyski, Erazm Pilz and Marian Seyda. Paderewski had been asked to take on the role of the KNP representative in the United States but he played no part in decision-making. The narrowness of the KNP's membership was seen as a weakness even by its leaders. They realised that it might have been wise to forge links with Poles in areas under German occupation, but they were unwilling to do so. As the war came to an end Dmowski feared that this might lead to the emergence of a left-wing government, something which he was determined to prevent.[4] Apart from the sheer difficulty of trying to communicate with people in hostile territories, as long as the war continued the Entente would have seen any such attempts as negotiating with the enemy; moreover, they simply did not know what was actually going on in Poland. Nevertheless Dmowski had no intention of entering into any power-sharing deals with the Socialists, and in particular he had no desire to work with Piłsudski, with whom he disagreed on the issue of collaboration with Germany and considered to be a dangerous Socialist. The only thing they shared was a deep patriotism and commitment to the Polish cause; they disagreed on everything else.

In February 1918 the French government and the KNP had signed an agreement to raise a Polish army in France.

This, however, became a source of constant quarrels between Dmowski and the French government, with Dmowski trying to use the issue of the Polish contribution to the French war effort to increase the influence of the KNP. When this did not work Dmowski had to think of other means.[5] He therefore decided to approach Paderewski with a request that he join the KNP. He was an obvious choice as the pianist's standing in the United States was enormous. Initially Paderewski felt slighted as he had also tried to form a Polish organisation in the United States, which he intended should become a provisional government after the war. He had also successfully campaigned for a Polish force, the Kościuszko Army, to be raised in the United States. He recalled: *There were moments when I was approached by my friends with suggestions that I form a Polish government in the United States... . I realised that I should not listen to this advice, though on several counts the idea was a tempting one. I maintained that I was a representative of the Polish nation which was recognised as such by the government of the United States. This was the only way I could serve the fatherland.*[6] But when Dmowski approached him, Paderewski agreed to join the KNP, thus giving it the appearance of a more broadly-based organisation. He considered all political activities in the United States to be his domain, though it is doubtful whether at this stage he anticipated assuming any political role after the war. The scene was clearly set for an unhealthy rivalry. United States government officials preferred dealing with Paderewski, whom they had come to know and respect for his contribution to the war effort. Colonel House and Paderewski had held discussions on the future of Europe, the results of which had been forwarded to the President. Paderewski's work in the Polish community and his calls for the United States to join the war against Germany were in line with President Wilson's policies. He was personally popular and had developed close ties with members of the American political and financial elites. Dmowski, however, was an entirely different man. His reputation as an anti-Semite preceded him and the Jewish community in the United States mobilised against him. Paderewski warned Dmowski of this problem when the latter decided to cross the Atlantic.

When Dmowski arrived in the United States at the beginning of September 1918 he had expected the war to continue for some time, as had many of the Entente leaders. On 13 September the two Poles were invited to meet President Wilson. By then the question had moved on from seeking American support for the Polish right to statehood to the much more complex issue of the future borders of that Polish state. Dmowski, bullishly convinced that he would be able to persuade American politicians with the strength of his arguments, delivered a detailed presentation on areas which he expected to be included within Poland. One of the contentious issues was territory which had previously been part of Prussia. Neither President Wilson nor his advisers were willing to give any assurances on that issue. Dmowski tried to persuade them to make a firmer commitment to the Polish cause by warning 'the position will be desperate unless Entente troops could come in and take the place of the German troops, which at least were keeping the Bolsheviks from gaining the upper hand throughout Poland'.[7] Unfortunately Dmowski's behaviour and his hectoring style made a bad impression on the President and his key advisers.

In the United States Dmowski came up against the political power of the Jewish lobby. Mindful of the fate of the Jewish community before the war, when the Tsarist government aided and abetted anti-Semitic outrages, and aware of Dmowski's racial theories, they expressed anxiety about the consequences of the emergence of an independent Poland. Their main concerns related to the possibility that a state founded on pronounced nationalist ideas would be likely to introduce discriminatory laws. What the Jewish lobby wanted was for the KNP to declare that it would protect the rights of Jews in Poland. Dmowski and other members of the KNP were unwilling to give such guarantees, claiming that this would amount to positive discrimination. The damage was done. Dmowski's association with the restoration of Poland had introduced a dangerous element into the struggle. In 1912 he had advocated a boycott of Jewish businesses. This and his racist and nationalist views meant that he, but also Paderewski, had been put on the defensive, trying to avoid accusations that were Poland to become once more an independent state it would pursue anti-Semitic policies. Jewish lobby groups called for the United States government to demand that the future Polish state should be obliged to make a prior commitment to respecting the rights of the Jewish community. Dmowski responded by claiming that the Jewish leaders wanted to secure special privileges which would in effect create a 'Jewish state within a Polish state'.[8] Attempts to overcome this potentially difficult situation by opening talks with representatives of the American Jewish lobby were unsuccessful as Dmowski insisted that they should first endorse his territorial demands, whereas they refused to have the issue of guarantees against discrimination made conditional on their commitment to an independent Poland. In the meantime, rumours of outrages committed by Polish and Bolshevik troops in border clashes increased Jewish opposition to Dmowski.[9]

Paderewski responded to the news of the end of the war with sadness. He felt this was merely an interlude before another war. His first reaction was to go to the British Ambassador and ask him what he should do next. He was told that he was needed in Europe and that he would be granted a British passport, since his original Russian one was no longer valid as the Russian Empire had collapsed.[11] Dmowski hastily returned to Paris, on hearing that an armistice had been signed with Germany on 11 November. He and Paderewski were only too well aware that his trip to the United States had achieved little but instead had stoked up mistrust. A commission to prepare plans for post-war territorial redistribution, chaired by Colonel House, had refused to accept Dmowski's claim that Poland should include areas that had been part of the previous Polish-Lithuanian Commonwealth including Prussia and Silesia. Nor did the controversies concerning his anti-Semitism go away; on the contrary, Jewish attacks on Dmowski increased.

> The war had come to and end. Armistice was declared. This was one of the saddest days in my professional life.
> IGNACY JAN PADEREWSKI[10]

Dmowski had abandoned a planned trip to Japan, where he had hoped to pursue his earlier idea of a Polish-Japanese alliance, but with the fall of the Russian Empire that plan was irrelevant. Instead he focused on the critical issue of securing the status of a provisional government for the KNP, in anticipation of the peace talks that were to come. As hostilities came to an end, Dmowski was only too well aware that the fight for real power in the Polish territories was only just beginning. Requests that the Polish army in France should forthwith be transported to Poland were ignored by the British and the United States. To Dmowski's fury it was instead decided that the German army in the East would stay in areas which it had held when the armistice was signed, for fear that a hasty withdrawal would create a dangerous political vacuum. Dmowski saw this as handing the right to decide Poland's future and its borders to the hated Germans.

Dmowski's efforts to ensure that the KNP would be treated as the first post-war government and would thus make all decisions concerning the new state were thrown into disarray when on 21 December 1918 he received a letter from Piłsudski who had in the meantime proceeded with his own plans back home. As it turned out, it was he, rather than Dmowski or Paderewski, who was able to establish real control over areas from which the Germans had decided to withdraw, namely the previous Congress territories including Warsaw. Dmowski continued to resist Piłsudski's overtures, justifying his actions by stating that 'some time ago I had come to the conclusion that Piłsudski was dreaming of a military dictatorship, of a Napoleonic role buoyed by revolutionary waves'.[12]

Paderewski and Dmowski had independently come to the same conclusion, namely that their hopes for the restoration of Poland would depend on the support of the Great Powers. But what neither of them had anticipated was the possibility that decisions made by the German High Command would mark the starting-point of the emergence of a Polish state. On 15 December 1917 the Soviet Government signed an armistice with the Central Powers. The peace talks which started a week later ended with the signing of the Treaty of Brest-Litovsk on 3 March 1918. The German army's anxiety about what was happening in occupied Polish areas was thus reduced. Though the German authorities had certainly had no intention of taking any notice of the various Polish committees which had sprung up in the West, they had had to consider the implication of growing anti-German feelings in the Polish territory they controlled. The Poles' desire for independence had increased. Strikes and signs of growing discontent within the Polish community were noted by the occupying powers. However, both the Austrian and German authorities had been able to retaliate, deploying troops no longer needed to fight against the Russians against the Polish workers. In the Baltic, Prussian and Silesian areas were inhabited by mixed Polish-German communities; the conflict became a civil war.

Piłsudski, who at the beginning of the war had believed in co-operating with the German authorities, by 1917 had come to distrust them. He accused them of making only limited concessions merely in order to secure Polish manpower. For this he was imprisoned for 16 months. Nevertheless, most Poles viewed him, rather than the more conciliatory leaders, as the true patriot, and support for him increased. Political parties began to position themselves to assume authority in a future independent state. As the focus of Austrian and German policies shifted away from fighting the war to the painful question of what would happen after their defeat, so there was less of a desire to hold on to Polish territory. Prominent Polish leaders, sensing this, took action to either take power or to at least stabilise the situation until a provisional authority was established.

In the ancient city of Kraków Wincenty Witos (1874–1945), a leader of the Peasant Party, formed a Polish Liquidation Commission. In the industrial centre of the Dąbrowa Basin, councils emerged claiming authority in the name of the revolutionary workers. The Austrian governor of the town of Lublin announced that he was handing all authority to the Regency Council, only to find out that Socialist leaders had decided to form the Provisional Government of the People's Republic of Poland. This survived for only four days, however. All these spontaneously-emerging authorities ultimately accepted that Piłsudski would be best placed to bring stability. He was expected to form an interim government and define and defend the borders of the new state.

Throughout Piłsudski's months of imprisonment in Magdeburg, as his prediction that the Central Powers would renege on their promises became a reality, the Polish community increasingly perceived him to be the true defender of their interests, and his authority grew. Once the German army faced defeat and news reached the officers of their government's decision to sign an armistice, so the initial plans to hold on to Polish territory were replaced by the desire to leave it to the Poles. The previously-established Regency Council was of no consequence. It too looked to Piłsudski. On 8 November 1918 he was released from Magdeburg and arrived in Warsaw two day later. The Regency Council hastened to appoint him Commander-in-Chief of the Polish forces. The German authorities were only too happy to accept this decision because Piłsudski gave an assurance that German troops, once disarmed, would be free to leave. Warsaw was liberated without a shot being fired and the Poles were able to enjoy the sight of Germans handing over their weapons and departing. However, in disputed areas, particularly those which had been part of the German Reich, the transfer of authority was far from bloodless. Local Germans fought with Poles for control of railways, factories and other strategic buildings. It would be some time before the ownership of these areas was settled and both the Germans and the new Polish authorities hoped to obtain international support to keep them.

Dmowski's absence from Poland was undoubtedly to

Piłsudski's advantage. The National Democratic Movement had been the largest of the political parties in Poland before the war. Dmowski had developed an ideology which most comprehensively addressed the issue of national self-determination and the place of nationalism in the future government of the state. In his interpretation, the concept of nation was synonymous with statehood. But by applying a crude 'biological' idea, he suggested that the formation of a state was the true reflection of a nation's strength, whereas the failure to do so showed its weakness. In the autumn of 1918 as the German and Austrian occupation of Polish territory came to an end, just how Poland was to be governed had not been resolved. In fact all the political parties, from the Socialists to the National Democrats had their own long-term plans. But for the time being military strength would determine who would be the winner. Piłsudski, as the man who had built up the first Polish forces, commanded the loyalty of the soldiers. The army was quickly expanded, the men who had joined the Austrian Polish Legions in 1914 forming the officer corps, and the rank and file coming from those Poles who had been conscripted into the Russian, German and Austrian armies. The German and Austrian armies withdrew from what were ethnically Polish areas but remained to support the German community in disputed territories. In the East the withdrawal of Austrian troops resulted in clashes between the Ukrainian, Belorussian and Polish communities. Although the armistice required German forces to stand fast in the East, from the outset Piłsudski intended to use his army to take control of the disputed areas.

The Regency Council had entrusted Piłsudski with the task of forming an interim government. He took for himself the title of Head of State, while at the same time acting as the Commander-in-Chief of the armed forces. His initial inclination was to ignore the KNP and Dmowski in Paris, though in fact the need to establish diplomatic relations and to obtain international recognition made this impossible. Although Britain recognised the authority of the KNP Balfour grew increasingly anxious about the likelihood of instability in Polish territory and was in fact on the lookout for someone else who could build national unity among the Poles, which he believed Dmowski was incapable of doing. The French government was less willing to see the KNP sidelined, however, since its headquarters were in Paris and there were Polish military units on French soil. The French refused to deal with Piłsudski alone, instead hoping that some accommodation could be reached between Piłsudski in Warsaw and Dmowski in Paris. As it turned out both of them did seek some form of reconciliation but for this to be successful one of them would have to back down. In December a messenger from Piłsudski delivered a letter to Dmowski, and during the following month the two conducted negotiations by courier.

At the same time Dmowski approved Paderewski's trip to Poland as the official delegate of the KNP. But there was much more to Paderewski's departure for Poland after so many years of absence. When the pianist's ship docked in London at the beginning of December 1918 the British government was waiting for him. The Foreign Office had earlier realised that events in Poland were slipping out of their control. The collapse of the three empires which had dominated the region, the revolution in Russia and the ensuing instability, all filled British officials with foreboding. There was also a feeling that Britain should not allow France to establish a firm foothold in Eastern and Central Europe. These considerations explain their grudging support for the KNP. But as the Foreign Office men reasoned, unfortunately 'in Poland, Piłsudski, whom they knew little and trusted less, had assumed a dictatorial role and called on a group of unknowns to form a government, without so much as a by-your-leave. It was an irritating affront to the Allies, but it was also, they felt, a dangerous predicament.' [13] The way out of it was to facilitate Paderewski's quick return to Poland and to encourage him to take up a political role. In view of his popularity it was hoped he would become Prime Minister in a Polish government. Paderewski's old acquaintance Balfour was directly involved in briefing him. After due consideration Paderewski went along with the British plan. Why did he do so? He was no diplomat and his understanding of politics was far from profound, though he was a Polish patriot and a charming man with the ability to persuade his listeners to agree with him. Above all else, he was vain. Years of campaigning in the United States with direct access to the most important people in the world, had all led him to overestimate his own role and importance. It is easy to imagine how little Balfour had to say in order to persuade him that Poland needed him. In Paris, Paderewski met with representatives of the KNP who supported his mission. Before his departure he had one last meeting with Balfour who told him: 'We have trust in you. We hope that you will do all possible to avoid the worst. We expect that your presence will prevent bloodshed.' [14] The journey to Poland was made aboard the cruiser HMS *Concord,* which docked in Danzig, which was still in German hands. Paderewski had insisted on this route in spite of British objections. The drama of his arrival set the tone for his journey and final arrival in Warsaw.

When the cruiser docked it quickly became apparent that the German authorities saw Paderewski's arrival as a political statement, which is presumably what he had intended. They tried to stop him from going on to Poznań, from where he was to travel to Warsaw. But he refused to turn back, even though a German chief of police ordered him to do so. The city of Poznań, its surrounding district and the port city of Danzig were in turmoil. Germany disputed Polish claims to its inclusion within the new borders and the local German community had taken up arms in order to prevent the Poles from establishing a *fait accompli*. Paderewski's arrival inflamed the situation by emboldening the Polish community, which took to the streets, demonstrating its allegiance to the great Polish patriot. On 27 December the situation became very dangerous as German *Freikorps*, consisting mainly of officers, decided to prevent the Poles from taking over the town. The hotel in which Paderewski, his wife and the British officers who accompanied him were staying was their main target and the pianist was forced to take cover when his rooms came under fire. This marked the beginning of an uprising staged by the Polish community to try to force the Germans out and take control. Paderewski was reported to have told the commander of the Polish volunteer units, *What you take now, will be ours*.[15] In reality the Poles could not ignore international opinion as the issue of the Polish-German border was due to be discussed at the forthcoming Peace Conference. Subsequently Paderewski's critics felt that he had stoked up conflict in the area despite knowing that it could not succeed.

Paderewski went on to Warsaw, where he arrived on 1 January. Everywhere crowds came out to greet him and this encouraged him to believe that he was not just a politician, but a man of destiny. As a famous performer he was used to adulation and public acclaim, but such was the mass hysteria surrounding his arrival that it was difficult to imagine that he would ever be able to assess the situation in Poland in a considered way. On the positive side, Paderewski forgot the fact that the initial idea behind his return to Poland was that he should act as the representative of the KNP: henceforth he saw himself as being above politics. This in turn, however, led him to overestimate his abilities and his influence.

The man who took most advantage of Paderewski's vanity was Piłsudski, who saw how he could benefit from the pianist's self-obsession. While Paderewski received delegations and attended meetings at which he was showered with adulation, Piłsudski got on with taking key decisions. In the first place there was a need to appoint a government. Piłsudski had absolutely no intention of handing over all decisions to the KNP and instead went along with calls that a government of national unity should be formed, one consisting of experts in their fields, rather than of politicians. Paderewski was only too easily persuaded to head this government. On 27 January 1919 he was appointed Prime Minister, Minister for Foreign Affairs and the Polish Delegate to the Paris Peace Conference. Few believed he was capable of even one of these functions, never mind all of them. But many knew that a difficult road to international recognition lay ahead and Paderewski was very well connected. It was widely known that President Wilson was a friend of Paderewski's and that he had met most of the prominent French and British negotiators who would have a decisive say at the forthcoming peace talks. Paderewski, oblivious to his shortcomings, *decided immediately, that in order to pacify the country two events were needed. The nation craved … bread and circuses.*[17] Food from the United States provided the first, while the forthcoming elections were to provide the second.

> **It was my mission to unite people's hearts and that I had to do quickly.**
> IGNACY JAN PADEREWSKI.[16]

# 5
# Paris

When planning the Paris Peace Conference, which started with a meeting of the Supreme War Council on 12 January 1919, the organisers were reluctant to give the smaller states the opportunity to veto their decisions. In due course it was realised that special committees would have to be appointed to deal with territorial questions and that technical experts would be called to report to them. These committees were set up between 1 and 27 February as the need for them arose.[1] In all cases, the interests of the Great Powers – Britain, France, Italy and the United States – determined the outcome of deliberations (Japan was officially one of the major Allies, but did not take an interest in issues outside its own sphere of influence). This is not to imply that the representatives of the Great Powers always knew what they wanted. In some cases it was admitted that information was lacking and in order to resolve some questions fact-finding missions had to be sent out and the information received had to be considered by specially-appointed committees.[2]

Events did not stand still during the Conference. On the contrary, as the great, the good and their advisers deliberated,

Eastern Europe was in turmoil. In the Baltic states the German *Freikorps* fought to prevent the establishment of Soviet control, and the Lithuanians, Estonians and Latvians allied with local White Russian units, the Germans and the Poles to resist the Soviet army. The Polish and German communities fought each other for control of East Prussia and the Poznań region. While the civil war in Russia offered the neighbouring states an opportunity to expand their borders, in Hungary a Communist regime came to power in February. This in turn led to revolutionary disturbances and direct confrontations with Romania, Czechoslovakia and the newly emerged Kingdom of Serbs, Croats and Slovenes (Yugoslavia). The Polish army was deployed in the East against the Ukrainian independence movement and the Belorussian and Lithuanian communities for control of disputed areas. Everyone agreed that by creating a *fait accompli* they had a chance to keep areas which they had seized by force. Piłsudski understood that only too well. He calculated that the Great Powers would have neither the manpower nor the resolve to reverse territorial acquisitions made at a time of international uncertainty. What he did want, however, was international recognition of the borders which he was settling through military conquest. Thus matters relating to the restoration of Poland were being fought on two fronts. In Paris Dmowski and later Paderewski set out to secure international approval for borders which were being defined on the ground by the newly-created Polish army. This created distrust of Polish motives at the Conference.

> 'The important point to realise about the Paris Peace Conference is its amazing inconsequence, the complete absence of any consecutive method of negotiation or even imposition.'
> **HAROLD NICOLSON**[3]

Initially Poland was assigned to the group of 24 states which needed to be discussed in some detail and whose fate was of particular concern to the Great Powers. Throughout their deliberations, their attitude towards Poland was far from fixed. For France, the question of whether to support anti-Bolshevik forces in the Russian Civil War meant that they would have to chose between their determination to set the clock back to 1914 and the Poles' wide-ranging aspirations to territory in the East. Furthermore, the presence of a Polish army in France and discussions on whether and how to transport it to Poland was a running theme in French deliberations throughout the spring of 1919.[4] As a result, the degree of French support for demands presented by the Polish delegation varied, though on the whole they were sympathetic. Lloyd George, the British Prime Minister, led a delegation which was firmly committed to the restoration of Poland to the map of Europe.[5] President Wilson, though in agreement with the principle of the restoration of Poland, left most of the detailed work to his adviser Colonel House. Japan had no interest in Polish issues, while Italy preferred to focus on topics that had direct relevance to its own interests, namely the Adriatic, Turkey and the Balkans.

The Polish case was initially discussed by the Council of Ten (the heads of state and foreign ministers of the five Great Powers, i.e. Lloyd George and Balfour, George Clemenceau and Stephen Pichon, Woodrow Wilson and Robert Lansing, Vittorio Orlando and Sidney Sonnino and two Japanese representatives who only took part in debates directly relating to Japan). This body emerged from the first meeting of the representatives of the Great Powers on 12 January 1919 and continued to meet until 24 March. After two months of inconclusive debates it was finally decided to reduce the size of the Council and thus it became the Council of Four (Wilson, Lloyd George, Clemenceau and Orlando). Because of the constantly changing situation in Poland during the two months of the existence of the Council of Ten, the Council created new consultative groups, either as fact-finding missions or as forums in which specific problems relating to Poland would be discussed in depth. In effect the Council of Ten made no final decisions on Poland. On 12 February the Council of Ten appointed a special Commission, chaired by the former French ambassador to Germany Jules Cambon, instructing it to prepare the Polish case but in particular to address the case of its borders. Its other members were W Tyrrell from Britain, the Marquis della Torretta from Italy, Dr I Bowman from the United States and K Ichiai from Japan. The Commission played a major role in negotiating and arbitrating in the Polish conflict with Ukraine over Eastern Galicia. In its final report the Commission made recommendations on the Polish-German border to the Council of Ten, but only then was it realised that its recommendations were based entirely on Polish submissions, since it had not been instructed to seek German views.[6]

At the same time the four Great Powers realised that the situation in Poland was slipping out of their control and that led to their formation of an Inter-Allied Mission in Warsaw to which they appointed their own representatives. Its main task was to exercise control over the ongoing Polish-Czech conflict in the disputed coal-rich region of Teschen. A Liaison Commission was appointed in Paris to process its reports, which were then forwarded to the Polish Commission.

The haphazard way in which the Council of Ten obtained and processed information was mirrored by conflicts within the Polish delegation. Poland was invited to send two delegates to the Paris Peace Conference. Piłsudski's first response was to try to sideline the KNP by sending his own delegation to Paris. When it arrived on 23 December 1918 it attempted to establish direct diplomatic contact with the French government. When this failed, mainly because the French Minister for Foreign Affairs Stephen Pichon supported the KNP, the delegation had to start talking to Dmowski. In the meantime Dmowski had made it quite clear that he did not recognise Piłsudski's authority as Head of State. Dmowski had tried to establish his own base in Poland by opening talks with the Socialist Prime Minister Moraczewski. The divisions between the two camps were very clearly defined, but the breakthrough came when both sides became aware that France would not budge and Piłsudski had to recognise that the KNP was well placed to conduct negotiations on Poland's behalf. On his part, Dmowski agreed to include ten members of Piłsudski's delegation in his Conference team. His co-operation was secured by Piłsudski agreeing to appoint Paderewski, who was at that time in Poland as the representative of the KNP, as the next Prime Minister.[7]

Dmowski was to be one of the Polish delegates and Paderewski, who on 17 January became Prime Minister and Minister of Foreign Affairs, was the second. Paderewski did not arrive in Paris until April, so in his absence Kazimierz Dłuski (1855–1930), a Socialist who supported Piłsudski, acted as Poland's second delegate. He more than any of the members of the Polish team disagreed with Dmowski's attempts to retain absolute control over contacts with representatives of the Allied states. Dłuski tried to reduce the KNP's authority and to make sure that the Ministry for Foreign Affairs in Warsaw made all final decisions. This led to a number of violent disagreements between Dmowski and Dłuski, in particular when

Dmowski tried to restrict his contacts with Warsaw. The fact that the officials in the Ministry for Foreign Affairs in Warsaw did not fully understand the rapidly-evolving situation in Paris played into Dmowski's hands, however. There was in fact a lot to be said for allowing the KNP delegates to take the lead in the Paris talks. Having spent the war in Switzerland and France, they had established contacts with the most important French politicians and military leaders. The Polish army in France, for which they had consistently campaigned during the war, had enhanced their standing. To replace these men with relatively unknown people from Poland, furthermore ones who had advocated co-operation with Germany during the war, would have been unwise and might well have undermined the Polish case. Dmowski dominated the Polish delegation which enabled him to ignore Piłsudski's preference for the reconstruction of Poland as a federal state. Dmowski did not agree with this and instead presented his own ideas to the Conference. In the meantime, Piłsudski concentrated on fighting campaigns on the Eastern borders.[8]

At the end of January Dmowski was invited to participate in the deliberations of the Council of Ten. Only when he arrived did he realise that he was expected to make a presentation outlining Polish territorial claims. Although he was unprepared, this was by no means an impossible situation for him. Even before his appearance before the Council he realised that this offered him a forum to present the ideas which had been the focus of his life. To put forward the case for Poland's existence, to defend the right of the Polish nation to statehood, would be the summit of his intellectual and political life. On 29 January he presented not only the demands and expectations of the Polish delegation to Paris, but his own vision for Poland which he had developed throughout his adult life. This was indeed the high point of his life. Unexpectedly invited to speak, Dmowski had no written notes. He nevertheless, by all accounts, delivered a lucid, well thought-out and extremely well-presented argument. All those present were deeply affected by the emotion shown by Dmowski, in what proved to be a defence of the Polish nation's right to exist. Since no official record was made of the speech, historians have had to depend on the accounts of those who witnessed it. He spoke for five hours but only well into his presentation was he able to use maps which were finally brought to the meeting room. When Dmowski real-ised that the translator was not up to translating from French to English he spoke first in French and then in English, thus ensuring that no detail or nuance was lost. Everyone was impressed with the performance, but whether they accepted Dmowski's argument is debatable. A member of the Polish delegation who witnessed Dmowski's presentation summed it up as 'not a speech, but a deed, furthermore a great deed, made by a Pole and a patriot'.[9] Perhaps the emotional impact of Dmowski's presentation led many Poles to assume that he had succeeded in winning over his audience.

Dmowski addressed two issues. The first related to the security situation. He requested that Germany should be forced to end military operations in Polish areas still under its control, in particular against the Polish insurgents in the Poznań region. This was an area that Germany insisted on retaining and indeed was allowed to administer pending a final decision by the Peace Conference. In January 1919 the Polish community staged an uprising which was put down by the German army. Dmowski then asked that the negotiators mediate to end conflicts between Polish and Czechoslovak units in the Teschen region. The second issue, and the one to which Dmowski devoted most time, was his explanation why Poland should be restored to its 1772 borders. Dmowski's key point was that a weak Poland would once more be the object of its neighbours' political designs. He warned that German ambitions in relation to Eastern Europe had survived their military defeat and drew attention to German support for Ukrainian and Lithuanian national aspirations. Dmowski dismissed suggestions that other national groups had a legitimate claim to independence. When discussing the history of the Eastern regions of the Polish-Lithuanian Commonwealth he asserted that 'the higher sections of those societies accepted from the Polish nation all values which elevated them above the peasantry; language and customs. Even the peasantry, which retained its own dialects, Lithuanian, Belorussian, and Ukrainian, absorbed a sense of loyalty to the Polish Kingdom'.[10] Thus Dmowski blithely dismissed the suggestion that these national groups were distinct from the Polish nation. His conclusion was that they were politically immature and would best be incorporated into a strong Polish state. He warned that were Poland not allowed to assume a stabilising role in the region, anarchy would prevail. Dmowski knew that his programme was at odds with the ideas put forward by the United States and the ethnic principle on which the British based their plans. Both delegations felt that Dmowski was wrong in rejecting the national aspirations of the Ukrainian, Lithuanian and Belorussian communities in order to justify the absorption of these areas into Poland. But in the long term, Dmowski knew that he could play the anti-Bolshevik card, in particular because in 1919 fear of the spread of Communist influence and the presence of the Red Army in the Ukraine and along the Baltic coast had created anxiety in Western Europe. Thus by presenting

Poland as a bulwark against the spread of Communism, Dmowski hoped to gain support for his plans. Even though many were impressed with the passion with which Dmowski delivered his speech, the final perception was that he tried to claim too much for Poland, riding roughshod over the aspirations of the local people. Interestingly, Lloyd George's account of the Conference reflected his greatest contempt for the French, whom he blamed for encouraging Polish greed. He accused the French of cynicism in using the general fear of Bolshevism to obtain their ultimate aim of a 'greater Poland'.[11] His grudging admiration for Dmowski's oratorical skills was confirmed by his statement that 'the Polish case was presented to the Peace Conference by an exceedingly able and cultured Pole of the name of Dmowski'.[12] This did not prevent him from concluding that 'the difficulties created by the unrestrained rapacity of nations that owed their freedom to a victory won by the tremendous efforts and sacrifices of the Great Powers, whose leaders were now engaged in trying to effect a just world settlement, were not a good omen for the success of a League of Nations'.[13]

During the weeks that followed Dmowski tried to follow up his presentation with written submissions. The Council of Ten and the Polish Commission were bombarded with memoranda. Of those, the one dated 28 February relating to the Polish-German border was undoubtedly the most important. 'The reconstruction of a Polish state should be considered to be an act of justice and a vindication for the crimes of partition,' he wrote.[14] He demanded that Upper Silesia, the Poznań region, Western Prussia and East Prussia should be incorporated into Poland. Although Dmowski accepted that Poland did not have a direct claim to East Prussia he suggested that the local population had been 'Germanised', which he saw as distinct from being ethnically German. Where there appeared to be no ethnic grounds for its incorporation into Poland, as was the case in Galicia and the Ukraine, Dmowski asserted that the source of conflict was German influence and that once incorporated into Poland, the local community would live amicably with Poles.

Initially it looked as if Dmowski had been successful in his policy of saturating the Commission with memoranda. The Commission's first findings were generally in Poland's favour. But Lloyd George changed the situation when on 4 March the British delegation started raising objections, fearing the long-term consequences of Poland expanding its borders. On 25 March Lloyd George delivered the Fontainebleau Memorandum in which he questioned the long term implications of a punitive approach towards Germany. He thus expressed doubts about granting France and Poland territories which had been previously German, fearing that this might cause resentment in Germany which in the long term might lead to political instability and even war. He agreed that East Prussia and Upper Silesia should be Polish but on 27 March floated the suggestion by the British expert on German affairs James Headlam-Morley that Danzig become a free city under League control, linked economically to Poland. At Lloyd George's intervention the panel of advisers was changed. Dmowski began to suspect that British objections were due to the influence of Lewis Namier, an adviser to the British Foreign Office who was a Jew from Polish Galicia. He interpreted these reversals as evidence of an international Jewish conspiracy against the Polish nation.

Paderewski arrived in Paris on 10 April, staying there until 8 May. From the outset he decided to take over responsibilities for all negotiations. Dmowski and the still extant

KNP delegation were supposed to accept their relegation to being Paderewski's support staff. Paderewski set up a new office from which he operated, rarely visiting the offices of the Polish delegation. To Dmowski and his team's irritation he never organised meetings to coordinate tactics and agree submissions. In his capacity as Minister for Foreign Affairs Paderewski believed that he did not have to consult Dmowski.

> 'And you the famous artist have become Prime Minister? What a come down.'
>
> CLEMENCEAU ON MEETING PADEREWSKI AT THE PEACE CONFERENCE.[15]

He eclipsed Dmowski and henceforth all documents and invitations were sent to Paderewski. Unfortunately, Paderewski did not understand how far the Polish case had progressed and showed no interest in working with his own delegation. Thus the two Polish delegates started working separately and not as a team.[16] On 5 May as the Commission on Polish Affairs was to discuss Polish actions in Eastern Ukraine and the Council of Four was to once more debate Danzig, Dmowski despaired of Paderewski's naivety. Writing to his friend Stanisław Grabski he stated: 'I can see Paderewski has no qualifications to lead a government. 1) He cannot make any decisions – he is afraid of everything. 2) In his relations with representatives of foreign governments he is too soft'.[17] But at the same time he warned: 'Do not try to overthrow him. That would do our case no good at the conference and it would cause confusion in the Sejm'.[18] In his memoirs Paderewski makes no reference to his participation in the Paris Conference. He mentions his arrival in Poland in 1919 and in the next chapter he writes of his return to concert performances. His critical contribution to the defence of the Polish case in Paris is passed over as if it had left a sense of unease or had been the cause of bitter disappointment.

We shall never know why Paderewski avoided referring to their conflicting positions during what undoubtedly must have been a critical period in the fight for Poland's borders. Was the great pianist driven by conceit or was his behaviour dictated by jealousy? While both emotions were likely to have had an impact on Paderewski's attitude towards Dmowski, the two men might have been divided by fundamental disagreements on what they believed Poland could achieve. Paderewski was supremely confident, socially at ease and vain. He nevertheless was intelligent enough to realise that it would require diplomacy and negotiating skills to get what could be achieved for Poland. Dmowski is usually portrayed as being devoid of personal vanity; nevertheless he was driven by an overwhelming sense of mission, a mission to which he had dedicated his life and which he believed himself to be absolutely capable of achieving.[19] A personal element crept into the picture with Dmowski suspecting that Paderewski's wife was influencing him unduly. He did not like her, even though he had been a guest at their Swiss home before the war. There is no evidence that Helena Paderewska had expressed any clear views on how Poland's case should be presented at the Conference or on the content of Polish submissions. What would have been deeply irritating to Dmowski was Paderewski's devotion to his wife and his public display of respect for her. Dmowski was partial to women's charms, but he had a deep dislike of strong women and in particular of intelligent and educated women who did not accept his idea of a woman's role in public life. To him a woman could only be either a wife and mother or a witch. When asked by a friend what Paderewski needed to do for a reconciliation to be effected between the two men, Dmowski responded 'poison Mrs Paderewska'.[20] This attitude only strengthened Paderewski's distaste for co-operation with the Polish delegation. It also explains why during the latter part of the Paris Conference negotiations were conducted almost entirely by Paderewski alone.

Dmowski and Paderewski both realised that Poland's borders and its place in the complex balance of power in Europe would be determined by the Great Powers, and in particular by the whims and foibles of the world leaders Wilson, Lloyd George and Clemenceau. These great men had convinced themselves that through their commitment to the restoration of Poland, they in some way had the right to determine the form and character of the new state. They thus proceeded on the basis that they were not so much accepting the re-emergence of Poland, but putting the country back on the map themselves. This meant that they were inclined to pay little attention to independent findings, expert advice nor the recommendations of the Polish Commission.

Paderewski's arrival in Paris coincided with the first major clash between the Polish Commission, which advised that East Prussia and Danzig be included in Poland, and Lloyd George. The differences between Dmowski, who in his irritation was prone to hector, and Paderewski, who relied on his personal influence, went deeper. Whereas Dmowski's saw himself as the defender of Poland's cause, Paderewski believed that he could charm the world leaders and thus by securing their goodwill, ensure that the Polish case was treated positively. As it turned out, neither was successful in persuading the three great men that they should look at Poland separately from their own interests. The result was that neither Dmowski nor Paderewski was happy with the final decisions and in fact both came to distrust the world leaders.[21]

Foreign diplomats and their advisers, on becoming aware of the friction between Dmowski and Paderewski, exploited it in order to drive them further apart and to weaken the Polish case. At that time Paris was hosting the most important international conference since the Congress of Vienna. The participants had a lot to gain and even more to lose in the course of complex and long drawn-out discussions and negotiations. Any sign of weakness in a delegation was seized upon by those who felt they could benefit from the situation. Czechoslovaks because of the conflict over the Teschen region, Ukrainian representatives anxious about the progress of Piłsudski's troops into Galicia and Jews hostile to Dmowski's ideology and deeply troubled by the rise of anti-Semitism in Eastern Europe all wanted to discredit Polish claims.

While Paderewski was initially sceptical of Dmowski's talk of an anti-Polish conspiracy, putting it down to the stress caused by the endless rounds of negotiations, he was quick to realise that there was a degree of complicity between the key negotiators, which looked very much like a plan to thwart the Poles. Paderewski clung to the conviction that all their problems could be resolved by interacting with the delegates on a social level, many of whom he had met during his touring years. In all situations he depended on being able to charm his listeners. Once in Paris, in quick succession he visited the French Prime Minister, the President of the United States and the British Prime Minister. Whereas Clemenceau seemed interested in defending the Polish case, Paderewski realised that Wilson was already shifting his attention from the details being discussed in Paris to the question of conflict-management in the years to come. Wilson told Paderewski that he did not think Danzig should be assigned to either Germany or Poland and that instead it should become a Free City. The precise implications of this were yet to be defined, but it was assumed that it would be guaranteed by the yet-to-be-created League of Nations. On 28 March the Central Territorial Commission discussed Danzig as well as a number of other territorial issues. At the meeting Wilson attacked Clemenceau over the Rhineland, at which the Frenchman walked out. The conflict between them resulted in Wilson taking it upon himself to resolve the issue of Danzig without reference to the French delegation. During subsequent meetings several thorny matters continued to be discussed, such as the ownership and use of the docks and how to force the German authorities to accept the proposed compromise on Danzig, but to all intents and purposes both the British and the US delegations were no longer willing to consider any other option apart from Free City status.[22] Paderewski tried to influence the British delegation's attitude through personal diplomacy and lunched with the British delegation and Lloyd George, an event which was a social success but which had few tangible results.[23] In the end, in spite of Paderewski's earnest appeal for Danzig to be incorporated into Poland, during which reportedly the great Pole wept, the Western politicians remained unmoved.

On 7 May the first draft of the treaty with Germany was put first to the Poles and then the Germans. On 16 June the final version was signed by the British delegation which had succeeded in cutting back some of the recommendations which had been generous to the Poles. Upper Silesia, an area rich in coal and steel production, was the cause of bitter disputes. The Polish Commission suggested that on ethnic grounds it should go to Poland, but Lloyd George disagreed, pointing out that its historic links with the Polish Kingdom were tenuous and that most if not all of the investment in the area was German. The final decision was that the matter would be decided by the result of a future plebiscite. The Council of Four, which now made all the decisions, was more obliging to the Poles on the Teschen coalmining issue, though this might have been due to the desire to compensate the Poles for the loss of Upper Silesia. The Poznań region went to Poland, as did areas between West and East Prussia forming a corridor to the coast. Paderewski and Dmowski's efforts to mobilise public opinion in favour of Polish demand by arranging for demonstrations in Poland and the arrival in Paris of delegations of Poles from the disputed areas were to no avail. The British were more concerned that excessively punitive measures would precipitate a revolution in Germany.

At the same time, events fast-unfolding in Galicia, where the Polish army was fighting Ukrainian forces, caused unease among the politicians gathered in Paris. Dmowski had no direct contact with Piłsudski, but nevertheless it was he who presented the Polish case for the inclusion of Eastern Galicia into Poland to the Conference. Paderewski, as Prime Minister and Minister for Foreign Affairs, should have had control over what the Commander-in-Chief was doing, but in reality he accepted that he had no direct control over Piłsudski and in any case he supported his plan for the incorporation of only parts of Eastern Galicia into Poland, including the town of Lwów (Lviv) and the oil-producing region of Drohobycz.[24] The result was that Piłsudski was given a free hand to establish control over as much of the region as he could, while in Paris Paderewski pretended that he was sending instructions to Piłsudski informing him to proceed no further. In reality there was a high degree of national consensus. At a particularly sensitive time in the negotiations concerning Eastern Galicia, Dmowski wrote to Grabski, a National Democrat colleague in Poland, urging him with the words: 'For God's sake, all of you should do everything possible to increase our military action. The whole of Eastern Galicia from the Carpathian Mountains to [the river] Zbrucz has to be firmly in our hands.' [25]

The Polish leaders were suspected of trying to seize territories where the Polish community was not in a majority and through that to create a *fait accompli* which the Conference could then be persuaded to accept. When accused of aggression, the Polish government and the delegation in Paris tried to present a case for strengthening Polish authority as a counterbalance to anarchy and the spread of Bolshevik influence.

The two main areas of conflict, though there were many lesser ones, were over the town of Wilno (Vilnius) and the fate of Eastern Galicia. The first arose due to separate claims made by Lithuanians and Poles. The former pointed out that Wilno was the ancient capital of the Duchy Lithuania, while the latter drew attention to its historic links with the Kingdom of Poland and the fact that the majority of its population was Polish. Both sides put their case to the Paris negotiators, but by then the Poles were confident that the Great Powers would not send troops to force them out. In January 1919 as German troops withdrew from Wilno, a Lithuanian Soviet Socialist Republic had been proclaimed with the help of the Red Army. Throughout 1919 fighting raged in the area. Poles fought the Lithuanians, who were themselves divided along political lines, some allying themselves with the revolutionary Russian forces, others hoping to establish a democratic state, independent from both Poland and Russia. In April 1919 Polish troops fought the Red Army to take over Wilno and Grodno. Piłsudski visited Wilno and promised its inhabitants that they would be given the right to decide their city's fate, but his troops refused to relinquish it. In the meantime, in Paris Dmowski, who wanted all Lithuanian claims to independence overruled, fought with Paderewski over the wording of the Polish submission. In the end the two delegates in Paris and Piłsudski agreed that Wilno would not be handed over to the Lithuanians. The Paris negotiators accepted that decision for the time being.[26]

The fate of Eastern Galicia was made more complex by the fact, that unlike the Lithuanians who could legitimately claim that they had successfully established a state of their own, the Ukrainian community was divided along religious, political and ethnic lines. The majority of the population of the city of Lwów and the area surrounding was Polish, but outside these enclaves the peasant community was Ukrainian. Most Ukrainians belonged to the Uniate Church, with a minority being Orthodox, while the Poles were nearly all Catholics. The towns also contained sizeable Jewish communities.

Before the First World War Eastern Galicia had been ruled by Austria. During the war Ukrainian nationalist leaders had thought of forming a Ukrainian state, to include Western and Eastern Ukraine. On 20 November 1917 a Ukrainian Central Council (also known as the Rada or the Directorate) based in Kiev had proclaimed the establishment of a People's Republic. At Germany's invitation the Council sent a delegation to the peace talks at Brest-Litovsk. However, German relations with the Council collapsed and its leaders sought support for Ukrainian aspirations from the Entente Powers. In the meantime, in Eastern Galicia a separate Ukrainian authority emerged, calling itself the West Ukrainian People's Republic. Its troops captured the city of Lwów on 1 November 1918. The Poles in the city, unprepared for this, were able to call on military units from Kraków. Although the Ukrainians were forced out of the city, fighting between the two communities continued with Lwów remaining in Polish hands.

This was the point at which the fate of Eastern Galicia became the subject of an inquiry by the Polish Commission to the Paris Conference and, after the signing of the Treaty of Versailles, the Conference of Ambassadors to which the matter was handed over. This inevitably led to attempts by Britain and France to settle the Ukrainian question in accordance with Ukrainian interests. As long as there was the hope of the Whites winning the Russian Civil War, influenced by Lewis Namier's suggestion that Polish claims to Eastern Galicia were excessive, the British feared that a Polish state in conflict with Russia would act as Germany's proverbial Trojan Horse. France, on the other hand, vacillated between supporting the White General Anton Denikin, who they hoped would head a Russian government after the overthrew of the Bolsheviks, and supporting the strengthening of the new Polish and Czechoslovak states as a barrier against Communism. A factor in French considerations was its growing interest in the oil reserves in Eastern Galicia.

Lloyd George now disagreed with Paderewski's claim that the Lithuanian areas, including the ancient city of Lwów with its large Polish community, should be included within the borders of Poland. The lingering suspicion that the nearby oilfield was important to the Poles created an atmosphere in which all Polish arguments were distrusted. When news came of clashes between Polish and Ukrainian troops, the Poles were instructed to declare an armistice. Paderewski was put in the personally uncomfortable position of having to tell his government that it was expected to cease military operations and that the national assembly, the Sejm, should not take decisions on the matter. Neither happened. Piłsudski continued operations against the Ukrainians and the Red Army which also had an interest in the region. The Sejm in the meantime declared that Poland should seek the incorporation of all the ancient Lithuanian Commonwealth into the borders of the new Poland. This was a highly provocative gesture at a time when the Paris negotiators were trying to assess the various claims to Eastern Galicia. In the end the matter was left unresolved, to be discussed later as part of negotiations for a treaty with Austria. The Poles nevertheless felt confident that if they continued to hold on to the region, no one would be able to unseat them.[27]

For the Polish delegation, the most unpleasant incident concerned the protection of minorities in Eastern Europe. Paderewski was only too well aware of the problems which could arise if this matter was ignored, in particular because of Dmowski's prominent role in Paris. He therefore reached out to the representatives of the American Jewish community who were the driving force behind this initiative and tried to reduce their anxieties. He also wrote to Poland urging the government to reduce the incidence of attacks on Jews. Unfortunately for all the small East European states, incidents of mistreatment of minorities, particularly Jews, were widely reported in the press. Paderewski supported the dispatch of a fact-finding mission to the East, but also tried to persuade the Council of Four that Poland could not introduce legislation which would give the Jewish community rights not shared by other Polish citizens. At the same time, anxiety was expressed about the future treatment of the German community within Poland. It was generally felt that there was a very real danger of mistreatment of minorities.

The minority issue was first broached by President Wilson on 1 May when, during a meeting of the Council of Four, he voiced anxieties about the possible mistreatment of Jews in Poland and Romania. At his insistence and with Lloyd George's support a special commission was set up to investigate the matter, though it was only to look at the treatment of minorities in the newly emerging states. This was then linked to talks on Germany, which was explained by Wilson as being due to the fact that millions of Germans were likely to find themselves living within the borders of the new Polish state. Only on 6 June was the Polish delegation consulted, even though by then the Minority Treaty had become an integral part of the Versailles Treaty. Predictably the Poles objected by pointing out that international guarantees for minorities amounted to a right of intervention in a state's internal affairs. Paderewski also pointed out that no country could allow the creation of 'a state within a state'. Reluctantly, because Lloyd George opposed Paderewski's arguments, the Council of Four accepted the Polish reasoning and modified the treaty. In the new form the treaty did not guarantee the minorities the right to complain to the League of Nations and at the same time reduced the state's duty to support the teaching of German and rights of cultural expression to areas that had previously belonged to Germany. Whereas the Treaty obliged Poland to respect the right of its German and other minorities, such a duty was not imposed on Germany. In the end Article 93 of the Peace Treaty with Germany stated that Poland had undertaken to protect the right of national minorities. The Minority Treaty was signed by Poland on 28 June 1919, at the same time as the Versailles Treaty. It acted as a model for similar treaties by defining the state's relations with its citizens. The basic principle set by the treaty was defined in Article 1 which stipulated that 'Poland undertakes to assure full and complete protection of life and liberty to all inhabitants of Poland without distinction of birth, nationality, language, race or religion'. The treaty made no specific reference to the Jewish community but by guaranteeing 'to assure full and complete protection of life and liberty to all inhabitants of Poland without distinction of birth, nationality, language, race or religion' (Article 2), the Polish government undertook not to discriminate against Jews.

The weakness of the Minority Treaty was the fact that it left the question of its enforcement unclear. Needless to say, the Polish delegation and later the Sejm which had to ratify the Treaty with Germany found Article 93 of the Polish-German Treaty and in particular the Minority Treaty to be an insufferable imposition. Nevertheless the Poles could not entirely ignore the President's request.

'Poland is an economic impossibility with no industry but Jew-baiting.' J M KEYNES[29]

Economic problems in Poland and the need for aid from the United States moderated any desire to be confrontational.[28]

On 28 June 1919 Dmowski and Paderewski drove to Versailles to sign the Treaty with Germany on Poland's behalf. In the Hall of Mirrors they took their place among the delegates of the Great Powers and other countries. When Dmowski and Paderewski ware invited to sign the treaty, they both appreciated that this was a momentous event for Poland. By calling the Polish delegation to sign, the diplomatic community recognised the restoration of Poland to the map of Europe. Both men gave the impression of having their vitality wrung out of them, however, having given their all during the negotiations.

# 6

# Unfinished Business

The first elections in the newly-established Polish state took place in January 1919. These led to the formation of a general assembly, the Sejm, which on 20 February adopted a new constitution. The National Democrats had secured the largest number of seats in the first Sejm but not enough to form a government. The other two major political groupings were the centre and the left-wing parties. All parties agreed on the need for a period of reconstruction. The first government had to deal with the pressing problems of creating the new state, the exact borders of which were far from fixed. The government could confidently assume control over the areas of pre-war Congress Poland which had been part of the Russian Empire, while the borders with Germany had been partially defined during the Paris Peace Conference. For example, the Poznań region, previously held by Germany, was now part of Poland. Polish claims to areas in East Prussia and Lower Silesia were to be decided by future plebiscites, and Danzig was accorded the status of a Free City under the protection of the League of Nations. Poland's borders in the East and South-East, however, remained fluid.

Piłsudski and the Sejm had calculated that Poland's case at the Paris Conference would be strengthened if the Polish army had control over disputed areas. But they had nevertheless been aware that they would need international sanction for any territorial acquisitions, and Poland would also need financial support from the Great Powers. The result of these contradictory considerations was that while talks were taking place in Paris and during the period following the signing of the Treaty of Versailles, Poland was constantly at loggerheads with the Great Powers and with the nationalities in the East, notably the Ukrainians, Belorussians and Lithuanians. However, the ability of the Great Powers to influence the Poles' actions was, in fact, only limited and in most cases indirect.

Political life in Poland was extremely volatile. The process of party formation was difficult and in many cases inconclusive. Politicians from the three different Partition areas had to form national party organisations and agree on an agenda for the first time. Not surprisingly this proved to be an impossible task as Poland was facing economic problems caused by the post-war slump and by the collapse of industrial production and trade. Poland was in conflict with all its neighbouring states. Between 1919 and 1939 Poland had 34 short-lived governments, reflecting the parties' inability to deal with insoluble problems.

When Paderewski returned to Poland in January 1919 he had no way of anticipating the problems Poland was going to face. He, arrived in Warsaw on 2 January. On 17 January he was appointed Prime Minister and Minister for Foreign Affairs. He resigned from both posts on 9 December 1920. His period in office was not a happy time for this sensitive and emotional man. In spite of becoming Prime Minister, his understanding of politics was limited and thus, inevitably, when he was obliged to resign, he scarcely understood why this had happened. Nor did he comprehend why politicians and the public had turned against him.

Paderewski saw his foray into politics as a vocation. But as it turned out, it became a journey of disillusionment. When Paderewski returned to Poland after signing the Versailles Treaty he fully expected to be feted as a man who had fought for Poland and who had secured the goodwill of the powerful international community. He believed that he had done no less than guarantee the creation of an independent Polish state. But the politicians and the people on the streets did not see it in these terms. They felt that it was they and the Polish army who had actually made the dream of a free Poland come true. It was they who had disarmed the withdrawing German troops, formed their own military units which secured key objectives and maintained law and order. As a result, Paderewski faced a highly politicised and increasingly vocal army, which had already proved itself in several campaigns. To many it was Piłsudski, rather than the negotiators in Paris, who was the real architect of independent Poland, a view which the man himself encouraged and to the creation of which his military comrades contributed.[2]

In spite of Paderewski's conviction that in Paris he had played a critical role in securing the best possible conditions for Poland, the view of those on the streets of Warsaw and in the Sejm was one of disappointment. He was accused of not having fought hard enough for Danzig. Its status as a Free City and the plans for a plebiscite in Upper Silesia rankled the

> 'I was nominated to be the Prime Minister of Poland. I told myself "This is the greatest sacrifice which I have made in my life".'
> IGNACY PADEREWSKI[1]

Poles. The Minority Treaties were also seen as an insult and an imposition. All in all, while Paderewski felt that he had done very well in the circumstances and that he had used his social connections to secure international aid for his war-ravaged country, all the Poles saw was a list of failed expectations. That their hopes had been unrealistic was not something any politician would be willing to point out.

In his five months as premier, Paderewski's status had fallen from being a man whose generosity and selflessness had contributed to the creation of an independent Poland to being perceived as a man without the backing of a political party, and thus lacking the ability to operate in the fast-evolving political scene. In other words he was seen as just an artist. When he came to Poland in January 1919 his mission was to reconcile the KNP and Piłsudski. It was the latter who wielded real power in Poland, and to whom most politicians turned in a desire to stabilise the volatile situation. The decision to ask Paderewski to form a government was taken by Piłsudski in agreement with the leaders of the main political parties in Poland. At that stage it was believed that the pianist's authority was such that he would be able to bring together the disparate political groupings and unite them behind the common desire for reconciliation. Piłsudski wanted to be free to pursue military campaigns in the East. This in effect gave Dmowski in Paris, still the leader of the KNP, considerable freedom in presenting the Polish case at the Conference. While Piłsudski and Dmowski vied for power in different ways, Paderewski, as the decent man, thought only of helping Poland.

During his first month in office Paderewski did little to dispel the notion that he was ill suited to tackling the problems facing Poland, namely the lack of a national currency and no state budget. Right-wing parties distrusted him for having

## THE FREE CITY OF DANZIG

The issue of the port city of Danzig offers an example of how during the Paris Peace Conference the Allies had tried very hard to resolve an issue but in doing so created a new problem, and one which furthermore became a constant cause of conflict between Poland and Germany.

The population of the city was overwhelmingly German, totalling 95 per cent of the community, while only 3 per cent declared themselves to be Polish. Nevertheless the city's historic links with Polish territories were obvious. Danzig lay at the mouth of the Vistula (Wisła) the main navigable river flowing through Poland. The city's prosperity in fact was wholly dependent on trade.

Those campaigning for the restoration of Poland after the First World War demanded that Poland should have access to the sea and Wilson's Thirteenth Point gave an explicit assurance that this would be the case. The obvious conclusion drawn from this and other assurances was that the port of Danzig would be incorporated into Poland with additional territory either from Eastern or Western Prussia. Nevertheless when it came to agreeing which coastal territories would be assigned to Poland the Paris negotiators started having doubts. Lloyd George in particular expressed apprehension about the incorporation of German nationals into Poland. In spite of Paderewski's passionate appeals on Poland's behalf the compromise solution fell short of what the Poles had hoped for. The city was designated as a Free City, that is neither coming under German or Polish jurisdiction.

Initially the city and the adjoining territory of approximately 1892 square kilometres was handed over to the League of Nations and briefly came under the control of a League body consisting of France, Japan, Italy and Great Britain. On 15 November 1920 it became a Free City. Though it obtained the right to self-government through an elected Senate, a variety of vague and ambiguous decisions allowed the growth of mutual hostility and claims and counter-claims between the League and the Polish state on the one hand and the Senate and the Polish state

distanced himself from the KNP and Dmowski, while those on the left wondered to what extent he had really broken his links with the National Democrats. He himself had no understanding of the nature of collective responsibility for government policies and instead of acting like a prime minister at the head of a cabinet, viewed them as he would an orchestra on the other. The city was separated from Western Prussia by a narrow strip of land which was assigned to Poland. The Poles felt that their need for access to the sea had not been recognised fully as they were only granted a narrow strip of land leading from the main Polish areas to the coast while at the same time they had not been allowed to have Danzig. They were allowed the use of port facilities which only further underlined the precariousness of Poland's situation. The territorial link, which came to be known as the 'Corridor', contained a majority German population who deeply resented being incorporated into Poland. While technically Poland had access to the sea the Corridor and Poland's commercial activities passing through Danzig were vulnerable to attack by Germany.

The status of the city was to be guaranteed by a special commission of the League of Nations. Unfortunately the attitude of the League to the problem came to reflect the attitudes of its key members. As the Free City of Danzig became a permanent source of conflict between Germany and Poland, the League members felt that they were made to uphold an unpopular arrangement. During the 1920s the post of League High Commissioner for Danzig was occupied by two Englishmen, Richard Haking and Mervyn MacDonnell, who refused to redress Polish grievances. The result was that the Poles came to see the League as the root of their problems.

After the Nazis came to power in Germany in 1933 the Danzig Nazi Party secured a majority in the Senate. Henceforth relations between the Polish authorities and the Senate became very difficult. When in 1934 the Polish and German government signed a Pact of Non-Aggression the Danzig issue was deliberately put on hold, only to resurface in the autumn of 1938. When relations between the two states broke down in the summer of 1939, Danzig was no more than a reflection of the enormity of the conflict, yet it nevertheless caused extreme unease in West European capitals as it was feared that the League would be forced to take action. This did not happen as the German attack on Danzig was just part of the general invasion of Poland.

there to support a great soloist. He appointed specialists and advisers, usually from abroad, as the whim took him. Since finance was the biggest problem facing the young state, Paderewski first considered bringing in economic advisers from the United States, but in the end appointed Leon Biliński as Minister for Economic Affairs. His expertise in the field was enormous as he had been Minister of Finance of the Austrian Empire before the war. Having done so, however, Paderewski ignored him and entered into private financial arrangements with foreign firms. Biliński's expertise was thus wasted and he soon fell out with Paderewski.[3]

It was well known that Paderewski was a wealthy man, though it was not known that he had a knack for spending money as soon as he earned it. Many of his personal ventures and investments collapsed, but the hole in his personal budget was always plugged by further lucrative engagements. Paderewski failed to understand that this was not how a government could operate. He frequently made decisions to order food to be supplied to Poland in the same way that one would purchase goods for a household. His rare consultations with the Minister of Finance led the despairing man to conclude that Paderewski was 'an outstanding patriot but a naïve baby in the world of politics'. When Paderewski resigned, it was reported that he had a personal debt of $6 million; money which he had borrowed from personal friends to support the Polish Treasury and which he never revealed to the government. In years to come he once more embarked on a gruelling international round of concerts. It was rumoured that he was obliged to do so in order to repay this debt. That money had been spent on equipping the Polish troops which were fighting on the Eastern borders.[4]

Once more Mrs Paderewska proved to be an asset to her husband, caring for him and making sure that he dressed warmly and took a nap in the afternoon. But not everyone appreciated her solicitude. In Warsaw it was rumoured that it 'was really Madame Paderewska who ruled Poland on behalf of or through her husband'.[5] She was known to interfere with his daily schedule, made sure those who would make undue demands on his time were kept out, and intercepted documents which might upset him. She too failed to understand that Paderewski was the head of a government and not an artist whose mood and health had to be protected so that he would be able to focus on his performance. She was perfectly capable of entering the room in which he was holding a meeting with government ministers in order to send them packing, in particular if she felt that the Prime Minister needed his lunch or a rest.

Not surprisingly as time went on, many, even those who respected Paderewski, felt that he was not up to the job and that there was a need for a change of government and with that of Prime Minister. Opposition parties responded to public anger against Paderewski over the treaty with Germany, hoping to gain popularity. On 5 November, Wincenty Witos, leader of the Peasant Party, declared: 'We hold it against the Prime Minister that his policy is not as independent as it might be, that he nearly always submits without protest to the wishes of he Coalition Powers, which often causes harm to Poland and lowers the prestige of the Polish state.'[6]

By December another issue came to dominate Polish politics, the crisis in Galicia. Piłsudski and other strongly nationalist party leaders found Paderewski's opposition to military action in the region irksome and wanted to get rid of him. After the failure of the Whites' offensive against the Bolsheviks in the summer of 1919 Paderewski had suggested that it was time to consider the possibility that the Soviet government would remain in power. Thus he thought that it would be wise to consider establishing some form of diplomatic relations even though there was no desire to grant the Soviet government full recognition. This went counter to Piłsudski's policy of making the most of the state of chaos in Russia to extend Poland's borders East. What upset Paderewski most of all, however, was the fact that while Piłsudski made a great pretence of defending Paderewski against his critics, he was in fact encouraging army leaders to attack Paderewski's policies on the grounds that they were likely to harm Poland's interests.

In December, having earlier survived several votes of no confidence, Paderewski finally informed Piłsudski that he could not form another government. By then Piłsudski wanted a free hand to conduct Poland's foreign policy and was only too ready to accept his resignation. In February 1920 Paderewski left Poland for Switzerland. He would remember his period in politics with bitterness. believing that he had been stabbed in the back. Nevertheless in his farewell speech he reaffirmed his commitment to Poland. *He who gave the nation his whole soul will not remain down for long, dead or alive, he shall be restored by the nation.*[7] His anger was almost entirely focused on Piłsudski.

> 'Poland's double policy, which manifested itself since last autumn, has created circumstances in which Poland's representative abroad cannot function without shame or humiliation. Everyone looks at us with distrust.'
>
> IGNACY PADEREWSKI, RESIGNATION SPEECH, 31 DECEMBER 1920.[8]

In addition to problems of defining Poland's Eastern border there were still a number of territorial questions in relation to Germany to be resolved. The issue of Silesia had been extensively debated in Paris but in the end the decision to grant most of Upper Silesia to Germany was not accepted by the Poles living in the area. During the period between the signing of the armistice with Germany in November 1918 and the plebiscite in March 1921, Germany was in control of the area. This led to accusations that they had used that period to bring in more Germans to intimidate the Poles. The presence of the Plebiscite Commission after the second uprising was not enough to ally Polish anxieties.[9] In August 1919 the Silesian Poles had staged an uprising in favour of the area being included in Poland. When this failed, in August 1920 a second uprising took place. Once more order was restored by German troops.

In the plebiscite in March 1921 a majority voted in favour of Germany, though the final result was affected by the votes of Germans who no longer lived in Silesia and by the inclusion of areas which had an outright majority of German people and thus were not areas in dispute. Germany and Poland disagreed over the interpretation of the results. France supported the Polish claim to the industrial triangle defined by the three towns of Bytom (Beuthe), Gliwice (Gleiwitz) and Katowice (Kattowitz) because it wanted to see Germany's industrial potential weakened. Britain, on the other hand, was swayed by the awareness that depriving Germany of its industrial capacity would reduce Germany's ability to pay reparations.[10] In the end, in spite of acrimonious accusations of fraud, the League of Nations upheld the majority decision for Upper Silesia to remain in Germany. In May local Poles staged a third uprising. The strength of Polish feeling against incorporation into Germany and French support for Polish demands led to a compromise solution whereby the towns of Katowice and Chorzów were granted to Poland.[11]

Poland's Eastern border was finally approved in March 1923. Policies pursued by the Poles between the signing of the armistice with Germany and March 1923 had a lasting impact on the way Poland was viewed by the European powers, on relations with its neighbours and finally also on the internal politics of the new state. In spite of Poland's borders extending beyond what was justified on ethnic grounds, most Poles believed that Poland could have claimed more territory, while the Lithuanian, Ukrainian and Belorussian communities nursed a sense of grievance and a desire for revenge, believing that Poland had been instrumental in thwarting their desire for independence.

Piłsudski had hoped to extend the borders of Poland Eastward. Driven by a desire to reconstruct the Polish-Lithuanian Commonwealth of the Jagiellonian era he envisaged a federal Polish state, which would include the Ukrainians, Belorussians and Baltic peoples. The problem with that was, like the Poles, they too had hoped for independence. Federation with Poland was viewed as denying them the right to national self-determination.

Of all the frontier disputes, the one over Eastern Galicia with its diverse ethnic and religious population, which had been left unresolved at the end of the Paris Peace Conference, proved the most complex. The Polish delegation in Paris had repeatedly tried to put the case for the region to be included in Poland, but as long as Poland's Western border was not resolved Piłsudski had had to proceed warily. Britain and France had accused the Poles of trying to pre-empt the decisions of the Polish Commission so they gave the appearance of accepting the arbitration of the Paris negotiators. After November 1919 when the Red Army effectively defeated Denikin, the French sought to find ways of allowing the Poles to retain Eastern Galicia, even if the British continued to oppose Polish demands.

At the beginning of 1919 Piłsudski's main worry had been the possibility of the Whites defeating the Soviets in Russia. The Whites insisted on the restoration of the Russian Empire with its pre-war borders, which threatened Poland's newly-established independence. Unsurprisingly therefore, in spite of British pressure, Piłsudski had refused to aid the Whites' fight against the Red Army. In June, General Denikin, who had been based in South-Eastern Russia, had launched an unsuccessful attack on Moscow. By October his forces had been defeated. Admiral Alexander Kolchak, who had established control over Siberia, was likewise losing ground by the end of 1919. General Nikolai Yudenich, who with British assistance tried to capture Petrograd in October, was also routed. This meant that the Red Army stood poised to move West and was likely to come up against Polish forces.[12]

Piłsudski hoped that the Poles would hold their own in the East. He had also been able to continue the expansion of the Polish army, since the newly-elected Sejm was willing to provide the money for his plans. Poland's drive Eastwards at the end of 1919 and during 1920 was decided on not by the government but by the military leadership, primarily by Piłsudski and those close to him. This in turn had an impact on Poland's foreign policy. Through the creation of *faits accomplis* Poland had embarked on a policy of confrontation with the negotiators in Paris, with the Soviet regime and with Poland's neighbours, Lithuania and Czechoslovakia. On 25 April 1920 the Polish offensive against the Soviet Union began. Initial victories in the Ukraine were followed by defeats, and the Red Army's victories brought it closer to ethnically Polish territory.

On 14 May Piłsudski authorised an attack on Eastern Galicia. The Poles were successful in their offensive against the Ukrainians but the French were angry at the use of troops which had been allowed to leave France on the understanding that they would only be used to fight the Bolsheviks.

Piłsudski claimed that he wanted to attack the Red Army and that he was not consolidating control over Eastern Galicia. This found favour with some Western diplomats who saw the advantage of allowing the Poles to capture the Ukraine just at the time when the Red Army was poised to move into the region.

Piłsudski had also been able to secure a military convention with Semen Petlura, the head of the Directorate of the Ukrainian Peoples' Republic. There was only one issue uniting the two, namely anxiety about the Soviets, who had made plain their support for a Ukrainian Soviet Socialist Peoples' Republic. On 8 May Polish troops and forces loyal to Petlura had entered Kiev, expecting that the population would support them. But the East Ukrainian population saw the Poles as enemies and considered Petlura a traitor. More worrying was the fact that the Soviet troops had not been defeated; they merely abandoned Kiev and regrouped, posing a danger to the Polish army in Belorussia, and the following month Semion Budenny's Red cavalry forced the Poles out of the city. In July General Mikhail Tukhachevsky defeated the Poles in Belorussia, forcing them to abandon Minsk, Wilno, Grodno and finally Białystok.

In Warsaw the government decided to seek the help of the heads of the Entente governments, who were attending the Conference of Ambassadors in the Belgian town of Spa. The purpose of the meeting had been to deal with a number of unresolved territorial issues between Poland, Czechoslovakia and Germany. The Poles were reluctant to negotiate directly with the Soviet government and therefore asked the Conference to mediate. Poland's actions in the Ukraine were condemned by the United States, France and Britain. When the Polish delegation, headed by Paderewski, who had accepted

a new position as Poland's delegate at international conferences, arrived there on 6 July they were left in no doubt as to
what Britain expected in return for undertaking to mediate
with the Soviet government: not only were the Poles to commit
themselves not to go beyond the Curzon Line (roughly the
Eastern border of Congress Poland), which the British considered Poland's ethnic border in the East, but they were to
give up their claims to Danzig, Wilno and the Teschen region,
the bone of contention with Czechoslovakia. Stopping on the
Curzon Line would have reduced Poland's acquisitions in the
East by defining the border as the river Bug and including
the towns of Białystok and Grodno in Polish territory. While
for the time being Poland retained control of areas up to the
river Zbrucz, the future of Eastern Galicia was made dependent on arbitration. The Polish delegation appeared to accept
these conditions but the Soviet government rejected British
mediation.

In August the Red Army reached the Wisła and threatened
the capital. During the following weeks, the Polish army successfully defended Warsaw. What is known as the Battle of
Warsaw even now invokes strong passions, with some seeing
this as a crucial defence of European civilisation. By October
1920 both sides were exhausted and agreed an armistice.[13] The
Treaty of Riga, signed on 18 March 1921, defined Poland's
Eastern border beyond the Curzon Line which irritated the
British but was what the Polish and the Soviet governments
were willing to accept for the time being. Piłsudski's concept
of a federal state, including Poles, Lithuanians, Belorussians
and Ukrainians, could no longer be pursued. The Belorussian
and Ukrainian areas were now divided up between Poland
and Soviet Russia. Poland retained Tarnopol, Rowne and
Baranowicze, but had to give up Zhytomir, Kiev and Minsk,

which had been briefly held in the summer of 1920. Lithuania retained its independence, deeply resenting Polish attempts to reconstitute the previous Polish-Lithuanian Commonwealth.

Nothing illustrates better the processes by which Poland's Eastern border was defined than the case of Wilno and the surrounding countryside. Dmowski firmly believed that Lithuania together with Ukraine and Belorussia should be incorporated into the Polish state. Piłsudski favoured a federalist approach in line with more liberal thinking on the rights of national groups. While accepting that the Lithuanians might choose to form a separate state, he advocated the inclusion of Wilno into Poland as a precondition for a settlement with an independent Lithuania. In Paris, Dmowski had tried to persuade France and Britain to support the incorporation of Lithuania into Poland.

The future of Wilno and that of Lithuania was closely linked to the course of the civil war in Russia. During the summer of 1919 Polish and Lithuanian troops confronted each other. The collapse of the Whites only further complicated the issue of Lithuania's future. Britain now became a champion of the Baltic States' independence from Poland. As Poland and the Soviet Union fought each other, the Lithuanians allied with the latter in return for Soviet agreement that they should get Wilno. The Red Army, on arrival in the city, initially refused to relinquish control. Nevertheless on 6 August agreement was reached that the Red Army would evacuate the city by 1 September, but Polish military successes in the war against the Soviet Union forced the Red Army to leave earlier and on 26 August the Lithuanians took control of Wilno. Under the guise of pursuing Soviet troops, Polish units pushed into Lithuania where in September they confronted the Lithuanian army. British and French condemnation of

Polish actions forced Piłsudski to change his tactics. Instead of openly pursuing his aim of capturing Wilno, he decided to pretend that this had been done by rebellious troops who refused to relinquish the city. By these means Piłsudski secured military control of Wilno and in 1922 its incorporation into Poland.

The issue of Poland's borders reflected a complex transition from the previous domination of the area by three empires to the principle of self-rule and nation states. The definition of borders, which ultimately was based on ethnic and to a lesser extent on historic grounds, was particularly difficult for Poland where there was an obvious lack of natural borders and where the border regions had always been inhabited by an ethnically-mixed population. At the same time, Polish disregard for the national aspirations of other groups caused friction and ultimately led to war. The emergence of an independent Poland inevitably led to local conflicts. Despite the passage of time, these were not forgotten, but acquired a deeply symbolic meaning, which had an impact on regional politics and thus on Poland's future foreign policy.

In October 1920 the Poles ostensibly agreed to leave Wilno in Lithuanian hands. Nevertheless on the 9th General Lucjan Żeligowski, having informed his men that he was no longer in communication with the army's high command, led a division of Polish soldiers into the town. Piłsudski's official statement was that Żeligowski's units had mutinied, although privately he had assured the General beforehand that were he to take the city, the Sejm would approve his action. Wild celebrations in the streets of Warsaw showed the degree of popular support for Piłsudski's policies. The Polish government's official statements that it had nothing to do with the take-over were not believed. Public opinion and the Sejm were in agreement and determined to defy international criticism. On 12 October Żeligowski declared himself head of the newly established Central Lithuanian State. He then created a provisional governing commission for the city of Wilno. On 8 January 1922 the city's elected assembly voted for the incorporation of Wilno into Poland, thus legitimising what was in reality an act of aggression.

At the same time Poland's behaviour alienated the European powers whose support it still needed. Poland was thus seen as an unstable East European state, one on which no security pact could be reliably based. In particular, this attitude prevailed in France, which otherwise would have been on the lookout for an ally in its desire to constrain Germany.

The political and economic problems facing the new state were formidable. The new states comprised territories which for over a century had been administered by three different Empires, each with distinct political traditions. Although during this period a strong sense of Polish national consciousness developed, one which transcended the frontiers of the three partition powers, the Polish state had to build institutions, establish a single legal code, a national economy and ultimately foster a consensus which would be a prerequisite for a viable democratic system. And all the while, the Polish people had high hopes that once independence had been secured, injustice, arbitrariness and poverty would somehow automatically cease to exist. Such expectations were impossible to fulfil and during the interwar period successive governments grappled unsuccessfully with the enormous problems facing them.

The wide-ranging borders which had been secured created a minorities problem. The first national census revealed that only 69 per cent of those living in Poland defined themselves as Poles. Over 16 per cent were Ukrainian and nearly 4 per cent Belorussian. Some 9 per cent were Jewish. At a time of economic crisis, ethnic conflicts were exacerbated. The Poles deeply resented the Minority Treaty which they had been compelled to sign and the National Democrats consistently campaigned against it, presenting it as foreign interference into Poland's internal affairs.

The biggest obstacle to the building of a modern Polish state and to the achievement of internal stability was the economy. During the years 1919–22 several waves of inflation hit Poland. In agriculture land reform was the most pressing issue. For it to be successful, the vested interests of the still-powerful landed gentry in areas previously under Austrian and Russian administration had to be broken. To do so the first governments had to be bold and determined. But political life in the new Polish state turned out to be unstable and was characterised by the a proliferation of parties, some of which were dominated by larger-than-life personalities. An example of this was the relationship between Wincenty Witos the leader of the Peasant Party-Piast and Stanisław Thugutt (1873–1941) leader of another Peasant Party-Wyzwolenie. Had the two peasant parties combined their forces they could have dominated the Sejm. This did not happen because Witos came from Galicia where the party represented the interests of the wealthy peasants and landowners, who wanted compensation for land which they were to loose during the land reform, while Thugutt was the leader of the Peasant Party which emerged in former Russian areas and represented the interests of poorer peasants who called for land reform without compensation for landlords. While Witos opposed Piłsudski, Thugutt's party supported him even during the 1926 coup. The result of disunity between the two peasant parties was that they never spoke with one voice in the Sejm. Lack of political experience and the leading parties' failure to arrive at a working consensus blighted all attempts to achieve any political aims or to address the country's very real economic problems.

In 1925 unemployment rose, prices increased and banks faced liquidity problems. At the time parliamentary democracy appeared ill-prepared to deal with the faltering economy. Many looked to dictatorships which had emerged in other European states as a model for overcoming both political paralysis and economic instability. Mussolini's example was seen by many as worthy of emulation. On 12 May 1926 Piłsudski staged a coup after the government resigned. The parliamentary system continued to function after the coup, but with increased militarisation of civilian life. The coup was presented as a moral renewal and a process of cleansing of the political life of corruption. In reality the military coterie, which came to dominate all aspects of Polish life while assuming the patriotic mantle, soon succumbed to corruption and directly contributed to the destruction of democracy in Poland.

Ignacy Jan Paderewski attending the first meeting of the League of Nations assembly in Geneva on 29 November 1920. Paderewski resigned as Prime Minister on 9 December 1919. In July 1920 Poland faced conflict with Czechoslovakia over the Teschen region and was in need of international support during the war with the Soviet Union. Paderewski was asked to act as delegate to the international conferences dealing with both crises. By December, angered by Piłsudki's decision to occupy Wilno, Paderewski resigned as delegate to the international conferences. In May 1921, realizing that he would have no control over Polish actions, which he had to defend in the League of Nations, Paderewski also resigned the post of Polish delegate to the League of Nations.

III

# The Legacy

# 7

# The Realities of Independent Poland

How does a marathon runner feel when he crosses the line? This question could have been put to Dmowski in 1922. He had dedicated his life to a single aim, the reconstruction of independent Poland. When on 15 May 1920 he returned to Poland, it looked as if he had nothing more to achieve. Everyone who met him during his first weeks back noticed that he looked older and appeared not to be sure what to do next. The fight had gone out of him. But this may have been due to the state of his health. In the autumn of 1919 Dmowski had come down with pneumonia. In those days, unless the patient was assured of the best medical care, the illness was usually fatal. Dmowski was ill for several months during which time his condition was critical on several occasions. He did not resume his post as Polish delegate to the international conferences which continued long after the signing of the Versailles Treaty, and was therefore not involved in the final stages of the talks concerning the conflicting Polish and Czechoslovak claims to Teschen. Nor did he participate in negotiations over the fate of Eastern Galicia, nor the plebiscites in East Prussia and Silesia. During the Polish-Soviet war he was absent from

Europe 1923

the international stage. Initially he had gone to the South of France and from there to Algeria. Only when strong enough to travel did he return to Poland. By then his contribution to the talks in Paris was easily overlooked. Poland was experiencing economic and political problems, which the politicians were unable to cope with. The diplomatic battles which Dmowski had fought in Paris were no longer relevant to the internal problems facing the new state.

On 18 March 1920 Piłsudski had arrived in Warsaw having conducted what he claimed to have been a successful campaign in the Ukraine. His triumphal procession through the city disguised the fact that at that very moment Polish troops were, after their initial victories, in full retreat. Nevertheless in March the people of Warsaw, unaware of the precarious military situation, wanted to celebrate. They believed that Piłsudski had fought for Poland's borders, was victorious, and in the process had rejected the humiliating restrictions which the European Powers had imposed on them. In contrast, Dmowski was associated with the frustrating and still inconclusive talks over Poland's borders. He was therefore ignored by many Poles, including leaders of the National Democratic Party.[1]

If Dmowski hoped that he could assume an important role in the creation of the new Polish state, he was quickly disabused. Piłsudski had no intention of sharing the limelight. Far from greeting Dmowski as an experienced and valuable colleague, he saw him to be a rival, and furthermore one who needed to be put in his place. Dmowski's hopes for a reconciliation with Piłsudski were quickly dashed after a meeting on 24 May. Dmowski had been kept waiting for an appointment and was again kept waiting when he arrived to see Piłsudski. During the meeting his offer of collaboration was ignored.

Piłsudski fully exploited the patriotic fervour which gripped all political parties during the conflict with the Red Army and the ongoing campaign in Eastern Galicia. The National Democratic Party was accused of ignoring the national interest and only being interested in winning seats in the Sejm.

Dmowski had decided not to take up any formal post within the party and although perceived to be the father and main ideologue of the National Democratic Party, he remained on the margins of the leadership. In July 1920, however, when the war with the Soviets reached crisis point, Dmowski was called to serve on the Council of National Defence. There he once more rose to the occasion. Unwilling to act as Piłsudski's poodle, he questioned the army's reckless actions in the Ukraine and suggested that the army leadership had misjudged the situation and had not conducted a prudent campaign. Such boldness was shocking at a time when the Piłsudski camp had successfully created an image of infallibility. To the suggestion that the army leadership had been responsible for military failures, Piłsudski retorted that 'a sick nation creates a sick army',[2] thus offloading the responsibility for the threat of the Red Army onto the politicians. Henceforth he would always blame military problems on those who criticised the military leaders.

The conflict between the two men came to a head on 19 July. Piłsudski threatened to resign – something he often did as he could count on this causing alarm among the other politicians who would do anything to keep him – but Dmowski refused to play his game. 'This you cannot do. You had got us into this situation, and you must get us out of it,' he declared, and then resigned from the Council and left Warsaw.[3] In July 1920 a coalition government was formed by Wincenty Witos, the leader of the Peasant Party, with the Socialist Party and the Union of the National and Peasant Party. The latter was an electoral alliance between the National Democrats and the right-wing peasant parties. Dmowski had opposed this and refused to be involved.

While it is easy to see this as a spat between two men with oversized egos, in reality Dmowski did not fit into the nationalist, jingoist atmosphere which prevailed in Poland at that time. This was a man of considerable intellectual qualities. During the war and at the Paris Conference he had mixed with statesmen and their advisers whose views were shaped by a profound understanding of

> 'Essentially there is no place for me presently in Poland ...There is a need to wait.'
>
> ROMAN DMOWSKI, SEPTEMBER 1920[4]

European conflicts, while in Warsaw, Dmowski faced a small world driven by petty intrigues. He, the architect of Polish nationalist ideology, was capable of presenting his theories on the basis of a thorough understanding of the European balance of power. What he encountered in Warsaw was a world so narrow that it was impossible for either Piłsudski or those who surrounded him to understand the implications of their reckless attitude towards Bolshevik Russia and the Western Powers.

Dmowski's withdrawal from political life appeared to be complete. He first went to Poznań and then purchased a large country house, which fully absorbed his attention. He admitted to feeling old and fearful of illness. The pneumonia which had laid him low after the Peace Conference had left him weakened but also henceforth prone to hypochondria. He had never married and there was not even a hint of him having ever developed any profound attachment to any woman. He was open about using the services of prostitutes;

on one occasion in Paris, he complained in a letter to a friend how expensive they were. To fill the void, he would attach himself to his friends' families and would virtually adopt their children. The extent of his withdrawal from political life was made that much more obvious when it was noted that he had shown no desire to be active in the National Democratic movement, the very movement that he had created and inspired through his vision of the nation as a separate entity. He had been elected as a deputy to the Sejm for a Warsaw constituency, but never attended any debates and even refused to declare his political affiliation.

Towards the end of 1922, however, Dmowski gave the appearance of wanting to become involved in politics once more. This was in spite of his speaking of his political career in the past tense. A colleague of his recalled that on several occasions Dmowski stated: 'I am not up to today's political battles. This is not the right task for me, others will have to conduct it, new forces, new type of forces.'[5] In August 1922 he declared his intention of abstaining from involvement in politics for at least three years. His stated reasons were poor health and financial problems, causing him to focus on his writing.[6] It is therefore difficult to fully explain why a man who only a few months earlier looked washed out and wholly taken up with his foibles and health anxieties, suddenly found his political feet and once more set the pace for the nationalist movement.

The next elections took place in November 1922. The National Democrats allied with the Christian Democrats (which came to be known as the Chadecja) won 98 out of 444 seats; not enough to form a government. This led the Chadecja to begin negotiations with Witos, the Peasant Party-Piast leader. The result was that in May 1923 the

National Democrats and the Peasant Party began talks on forming a government which they did in October, though the result was a highly unstable coalition. At the same time another battle was fought over the elections to the presidency, scheduled for early December 1923. Piłsudski, angry that the recently-approved constitution granted the President little authority, declared that he would not stand. These factors might account for Dmowski's willingness at the end of 1922 to review his only recently stated desire to withdraw from politics. One possible reason is that he saw an opportunity to sideline Piłsudski. By then the rivalry between the two men had become public knowledge and there was no chance of any reconciliation. The other explanation is more interesting and likely to be the more credible. News of developments in Italy appears to have galvanised the younger members of the nationalist movement. The Fascists' successes in entering national politics and their so-called 'March on Rome' which conveyed a sense of purpose and national pride all found ready echoes in the hearts of young Poles, in particular those who wanted to confront left-wingers and striking workers in the streets. Dmowski liked what he heard of the Fascists and began to consider modelling the nationalist movement on them. He had also come to the conclusion that the National Democrats had been ineffective in politics and needed a transfusion of young blood.

The national emergency caused by deep social divisions and in particular waves of strikes, which started in 1923, led many politicians to consider Dmowski as a partner in government. Witos's Peasant Party-Piast was seen as right-wing and representing the interests of the wealthy peasants, especially those opposed to unity with the radical workers, and saw advantages in co-operation with the National Democrats.

When in October 1923 the two parties formed a government, Dmowski re-entered politics by agreeing to act as Minister for Foreign Affairs. His period in office turned out to be brief, no more than six weeks. Nevertheless during that time he dealt with a number of foreign policy issue, most important of which was the conclusion of talks with the Soviet Union, as a result of which it recognised Poland.

The government fell in December 1923 when it failed to agree on how to deal with mounting social tensions caused by the economic collapse. The leadership of the National Democratic Party advocated confronting the strikers and the Socialist Party. Witos was reluctant to do this and in any case he was more worried about the lot of the peasants, who had been hit equally hard by the crisis. This led to the collapse of the coalition. Once more Dmowski returned to writing and showed a lively interest in world affairs. Soon he was again writing articles in *Przegląd Wszechpolski*, a weekly magazine connected with the nationalist movement. In 1924 he completed a book entitled *Polish Politics and the rebuilding of a state*. Some have suggested that the impetus for finishing the book came when Piłsudski published his memoirs under the title of *The Year of 1920*. Dmowski was so irritated by it that he decided to offer his own analysis of Poland's position in Europe. Many in Poland, including those not connected with the nationalist movement, considered Dmowski to be very well placed to give an overview of the situation, in particular because Poland's relations with European states were still characterised by insecurity and anxiety about further border conflicts.

As always, the key question for Dmowski was Poland's position between Germany and Russia. He expressed anxiety that the Treaty of Versailles had not weakened Germany enough and that through its uncompromising policies the Weimar Republic was becoming the pariah of Europe. His analysis of the Soviet Union was surprisingly lacking in right-wing rhetoric. He considered it to be a weak state, while fearing that Germany had the potential to once more dominate Central Europe. Dmowski believed Germany would continue its anti-Polish policies and since Poland could not fight a war on two fronts, he believed the conflict with Germany should take priority and that good relations should be sought with the Soviet Union. This went against the general trend of Polish opinion which saw Russia as the greatest threat.

Dmowski never abandoned his anti-Semitic opinions and in articles and the book published in the 1920s he reiterated that the Jews were the enemies of the Polish nation. While he was surprisingly balanced in his analysis of Poland's foreign policy, his hatred of Jews rendered him incapable of any rational assessment of the subject and he remained convinced that the Jews were responsible for all Poland's misfortunes.

After the Witos government fell in December 1923, a non-party government led by Władysław Grabski was formed, lasting until November 1925. Grabski's main aim was to stabilise the economy and to reform state finances. In this he initially succeeded and his government created the conditions for a brief period of stability. Unfortunately by the beginning of 1925 the economy and state finances were once more in disarray. The German government's tariff war against Poland, intended to destroy the Polish economy, succeeded in causing major upheavals. In 1925 Dmowski and the National Democratic Party started to consider a coup. It had been rumoured that Dmowski was involved in planning for the overthrow of the parliamentary system, which was seen as too weak and incapable of coping with the economic and social conflicts bedevilling Poland. The question was, if the coup succeeded, to whom would the role of acting as the country's benevolent dictator be entrusted. Becoming a Polish Mussolini was not Dmowski's style and Piłsudski was too independent-minded. Thus, General Władysław Sikorski, who had been Minister of War in the 1923/4 government, was approached. At the same time, the National Democrats began portraying Paderewski as the only man who could still oppose Piłsudski. It is difficult to say for certain if such plans were made or whether it merely suited the National Democrats to spread such rumours.[7] Whatever the case, the plans, if they existed, came to nothing and within a year, on 12 May 1926, Piłsudski staged a coup himself.

Piłsudski claimed he was acting against a political system that allowed parties to use the Sejm to pursue their own agenda, rather than serve the interests of the nation. The main object of his attack was the coalition government formed by Witos and the National Democrats on 5 May 1926. Earlier he had accused the ruling Peasant Party of corruption. In a widely publicised

**Władysław Sikorski** was born in 1881 in Austrian-controlled Galicia. He chose a military career after attending the Austrian Military School. Jointly with Piłsudski he organised the Riflemen's Association which the Austrian government encouraged before the First World War. When Piłsudski agreed to form Polish legions to fight with Germany and Austria against Russia, Sikorski was one of his closest comrades. They nevertheless fell out when Piłsudski refused to go along with German plans. Henceforth the two remained estranged. In 1922 Sikorski became Prime Minister. In 1926 he refused to participate in the coup, something Piłsudski and his supporters never forgave him for. He was removed from active service and spent his time studying military doctrine in France. In 1936 he became a vocal critic of the military regime which maintained a grip on power after Piłsudski's death. When Germany attacked Poland in September 1939 Sikorski decided to go to France. There in the face of strong opposition from the Piłsudski group, he was able to form a government in exile. He died in a tragic air accident off Gibraltar on 4 July 1943.

article which appeared on 20 April he threatened that the army would act if the Peasant Party and the National Democrats formed a government. He accused the National Democrats, more than any other party, of abusing power for their own selfish ends. In reality Poland faced industrial and agricultural problems and needed reforms, which no party was willing to implement, fearful of alienating the electorate. The idea of rule by a strong man, independent of the Sejm, dedicated to salvaging the economy and to creating national unity found ready support in a society racked by such problems.

Fearing that the National Democrats were about to form the next government, many parties, including the Socialist Party, supported Piłsudski. In the fighting with troops loyal to the President 379 people died. Surprisingly, Piłsudski kept out of the new government, which was instead led by the non-partisan figure of Kazimierz Bartel (1882–1941). However, Piłsudski was elected President on 31 May. He nevertheless refused to accept the post as he realised it would not give him the extensive political influence he sought. Instead in October 1926 he became Prime Minister.

Dmowski had been in Paris when the coup took place and he rushed back to Poland. There he found his old adversary triumphant. Piłsudski declared 'It is not the question of left or right ... [I] am not of the left, nor for the left, I am for my countrymen ... People's government!'[8] Hand-picked by Piłsudski, the members of the government moved swiftly to introduce constitutional amendments which reduced the authority of the Sejm. By ensuring that he was appointed as Minister of War and Inspector-General of the Armed Forces Piłsudski retained absolute control over military affairs, although in fact he retained absolute control over all government policy.

The setback suffered by the National Democrats forced Dmowski to reflect on just what had been the advantages of participating in the democratic process and on the decision to collaborate with the peasant movement. Piłsudski's successful coup and the support given to him by the left and centre parties called for serious consideration. Dmowski was finally fully mobilised and on 4 December of the same year he announced the formation of a new organisation called the Camp for Greater Poland (OWP). In the long term he intended to overthrow the Piłsudski regime by consolidating all parties and organisations which defined themselves as belonging to the nationalist camp, which included the National Democrats, Christian parties, some of the peasant parties, Christian trade unions and youth organisations. While at the time of its launch the OWP tried to present itself as a patriotic organisation which was above party politics, in the long term it was hoped that it would act as a disciplined nationalist force. However, the disunity and internal conflicts characteristic of the nationalist movement made this impossible.[9]

From the outset the organisation was rigidly hierarchical with no pretence of democracy. Members of the organisation were to accept discipline and obey orders. Only Catholics would be accepted as members, who had to swear to serve the nation and uphold Catholic values and Polish traditions. Dmowski became Chairman of the Supreme Council of the OWP. Great stress was put on youth and the need for a renewal of the nationalist movement, which became more important when in the 1928 elections the Nationalists lost two-thirds of their seats. The nationalist parties were in retreat, confounded by Piłsudski's policies of moving away from the left and centre parties which had earlier supported him and forming tactical alliances with the landowners, industrialists and financiers.

'The nation state should be a nation which is organised,' Dmowski wrote.[10] Although many young people within the OWP saw Italian fascism as a model, Dmowski still disagreed. The OWP was not to be a revolutionary or even a radical movement, which was how the Italian Fascists portrayed themselves. Nor did he like the idea of a bloated state structure which would act as a means of enforcing party rather than national discipline. Although he was always impressed by the vitality and energy generated by the Fascist movement, he noted that the state created in Italy lacked solid legal foundations. However, in 1929–30 nationalist youth flocked to the ranks of the OWP and affiliated organisations, leading to problems as these younger members challenged decisions made by the leadership. Many felt that Dmowski should now throw in his lot with Piłsudski, who was attacking the Socialists, Communists, trade unionists and left-wing organisations. Others felt that Dmowski should be clearer about his rejection of parliamentary democracy and give the signal for the organisation to take to the streets. Dmowski did neither, which in due course led to divisions within the OWP.[11]

In July 1928 Dmowski presided over the creation of a new party, the Nationalist Alliance (SN). The Nationalists were now divided, youth activities being concentrated in the OWP and parliamentary work in the SN, although Dmowski remained firmly in control of both organisations. There was an inherent weakness in his monopoly of all decision-making within the nationalist movement. Poland was hard hit by the Great Depression in 1929, and Dmowski concluded that the Piłsudski regime would collapse and that the nationalist movement would simply assume power, rather than have to fight for it. This explains his unwillingness to go beyond rhetoric about bringing down the regime. The nationalist movement would therefore not unite with the Socialists and the centre parties in an anti-Piłsudski coalition, which allowed the regime to continue unchallenged.

In January 1928 a Non-Party Bloc of Co-operation with the Government had been formed to bring together all sections of society. In effect it was an attempt to undermine the other political parties, particularly the National Democrats, and to create a party which represented the interests of the regime. Having initially put out feelers to the OWP the Piłsudski regime had decided to launch an all-out attack on Dmowski. He was put under close surveillance and was followed everywhere by the police. Whenever he made a speech or attended a meeting, police and troops waited outside anticipating a riot. On more than one occasion it was suspected that the police were trying to provoke violence. In September 1930 the government imposed emergency laws and arrested all opposition party leaders including many from the nationalist movement. Dmowski was not arrested but the OWP was on the defensive. The government proceeded to undermine the Sejm and to limit civil rights. Officers in uniform would enter the Sejm, disrupt debates and even beat up the deputies. The judiciary was reformed, so that new judges were more obliging to the regime. Legislation was introduced limiting the rights to free association and political activity. All these measures were aimed at the National Democrats and Dmowski, who continued to be seen as the only politician capable of challenging Piłsudski. In March 1933 the government disbanded the OWP, which it saw as a rival to its attempts to form its own party. The young nationalists, who had been initially attracted to the organisation because of its aggression and promise of action, felt thwarted by the old leadership and formed their own nationalist organisation,

the National-Radical Camp (ONR). The authorities immediately declared it illegal, which merely drove it underground
where it continued to function as a terrorist group. Dmowski
dissociated the nationalist movement from its activities.

During the first half of the 1930s Dmowski once more
focused on his writing and four of his major works appeared
during this period. His main preoccupation was the state of
the economy, the Nazi and Fascist parties in power and the
relationship between the Catholic Church and nationalism.
In retrospect it is surprising to note that he disapproved of
growth of the radical right in Europe. Since his theories on
European political developments usually came back to the
question of Poland's place in Europe he continued to express
deep anxiety about the growth of Germany's power. While
he was in many ways perceptive in his analysis of the lack
of legality and lack of proper state institutions in Italy and
Germany, his obsession with Jewish and Masonic conspira-
cies blinded him to the full implications of what was happening in Germany. Thus Dmowski believed that whereas initially
German and Jewish groups conspired to destroy Poland, were
the power of the Jewish community to be destroyed by the
Nazis, Germany would become less of a threat to Poland
thanks to the removal of Jewish influence over its policies.

Dmowski was an observant Catholic and a firm believer
in the spiritual connection between the Polish nation and the
Church. He was nevertheless capable of assessing its useful-
ness from a clearly political perspective. Thus when discussing the role of the Church in preventing Poles from being
attracted to Socialist and Communist movements he did not
think there was any need to fight for enlightenment and education. 'I have faith in Poland as long as there are illiterate
people here,' he said.[12] Consummate politician that he was,

he knew the power of simple slogans which at their briefest and most effective were confined to the call 'for God and the Fatherland'. Nevertheless, Dmowski's distrust of party politics led him to advocate that the Catholic Church should not be involved in politics of the nation as it would lose its role as the spiritual guide of the nation as a result.

On 12 May 1935 Piłsudski died. He left no natural successor and it was widely anticipated that the military junta which had ruled Poland would succumb to internal conflicts and collapse. In an article which appeared immediately after Piłsudski's death Dmowski wrote that 'an obvious fact has to be stated that the role he had played creates at the time of his death an opportunity of great importance'.[13] Many saw in this a call for the nationalist movement to seize power, though Dmowski claimed to be merely stating the obvious. The authorities confiscated the newspapers in which the article appeared, but his phrase nevertheless captured the mood of foreboding which affected Poland. An eclipse of the sun which followed Piłsudski's death and unusual cloud formations during the funeral increased the mood of public apprehension. Still Dmowski refused to take the lead, instead repeating the old formula that the regime would collapse and that power would fall into the nationalists' laps. This did not happen as the regime regrouped and what followed was the formation of a government based on the military, with the national assembly uneasily coexisting with the powerful military leadership, and which came to be known as the 'Rule of the Colonels'.

Dmowski's timidity in the face of this apparent political opportunity may be explained by the state of his health. Piłsudski's death reminded him forcefully of his own mortality. Indeed, there was a lot to worry about. In 1934 in spite of a long convalescent trip to Algeria his health deteriorated.

He also faced financial difficulties and had to sell his country house near Poznań. To his embarrassment he found that he was unable to pay off all his debts. Henceforth his only source of income was writing but by the mid-1930s ill-health prevented him from continuing with his hitherto prolific work. Only the support of his friends saved him from ruin.

In 1936 Dmowski's brother, the only other surviving member of his family, died. His predisposition to anxiety about his health and general sense of despondency increased. He stopped writing and no longer took walks in the country, which until then had been his passion. When in the spring of 1937 he suffered a minor brain haemorrhage his physical and mental state deteriorated further. Throughout this period, since he had been forced to sell his country house, Dmowski had lived with the Niklewicz family whom he had known since he first became active in politics. They were his surrogate family throughout his adult life. By March of the following year it was obvious that he was incapable of taking part in any political activities. From the summer of 1938 he was no longer aware of his surroundings and his mind wandered. His death was not unexpected as during the winter he developed pneumonia and his heart was visibly failing. On 2 January 1939 Dmowski died.

His body was taken to Warsaw where the coffin was displayed in the cathedral. He was buried in the family grave in Bródno. When Dmowski's coffin was conveyed through Warsaw a crowd of some 100,000 people came out onto the streets to pay their respects. The nationalist movement intended this to be a demonstration of its strength and a challenge to the government. For its part, the government ensured that its disapproval of Dmowski was made public by not sending a representative to the funeral.

An intriguing postscript to Dmowski's burial is given by the Primate of Poland's rumoured refusal to allow his body to be buried in the Warsaw cathedral vaults. During the funeral orations his supporters and admirers drew attention to his long commitment to the Polish cause, the high point of which was the defence of Polish interests during the Paris Peace Conference. While abroad he was remembered as a statesman, the Polish government of the time, a ruling military coterie. He was the man who maintained silence and chose to ignore what undoubtedly was a distinguished, albeit always controversial, contribution to the Polish cause. It was reported that his last words were '... already they cannot understand me'.[14]

# 8

# The Return to the Piano

*I have realised that public speaking is more inspiring than playing. And now I think that the most interesting is to have both these experiences behind you.*[1] This is how Paderewski described his feelings for the two activities which dominated his life. In February 1920, when Paderewski left Poland after his ignoble dismissal from the premiership, it looked as if his political and musical years were behind him. On leaving the government Paderewski requested to be relieved of his responsibility as delegate to the Paris Conferences. He had been vilified in Poland for having signed what was believed to be an unfavourable territorial treaty with Germany, after which he decided he would have no more to do with Polish politics. But he did not plan to return to the piano, or even believe it was possible to do so. He had not touched a keyboard for ten years and even earlier he had medical and psychological problems, which made playing difficult.

But as Paderewski, his beloved wife and their entourage arrived at his house near Geneva he immediately had to face the fact that he was in financial difficulties. Until the outbreak of the war Paderewski had spent freely. He had a large household to support and he was notoriously generous to many charities. Nevertheless he had always been able to earn more money by touring, so the war, when he stopped playing and instead devoted himself to the Polish cause, put a heavy strain on his finances. In any case, Paderewski had to face the obvious fact that he was not particularly good at handling the money he earned. This raised the difficult question of where his future earnings would come from. None of his investments, not even prospecting for oil on the farm in California he had bought before the war, were profitable. All attempts to raise loans were equally unsuccessful. This left him with only one option and that was to return to concert performances. But before he could concentrate on regaining his old skills, a call came from the government to once more act as ambassador for the Polish cause. In spite of his earlier anger and declarations that he was done with politics, Paderewski accepted the position; he knew Poland needed him.

In years to come, after Paderewski had done all in his power to defend Polish interests at international conferences and when he, in hindsight, had realised that he could not have done more, he would bitterly regret his decision. *When Poland was reborn it was its misfortune, that at the cradle stood two madmen, Piłsudski and Dmowski*, he declared.[2] The reason for this was that Paderewski, as we have seen, was drawn into resolving the conflict with the Soviet Union, which had begun with Piłsudski's Ukrainian offensive in April 1920. Facing defeat by the Red Army, the Polish government had asked the Conference of Ambassadors in Spa to broker a peace agreement between Poland and the Soviet Union. Paderewski then found himself having to accept the humiliating terms proposed, under which Poland would lose disputed territories to Czechoslovakia and also the port of Danzig.

The cynical nature of the government's ploy in offering him the role was made obvious when it became clear that while Paderewski was to defend, cajole and plead for Poland at the international conferences and in the League of Nations, in Poland Piłsudski continued to pursue his foreign policy objectives in the East through military force. The fact that Britain and France were willing to use Poland's moment of military weakness to renegotiate agreements on territorial issues not connected with the Polish-Soviet conflict made Paderewski equally bitter and disillusioned with the Great Powers. On 14 December he tendered his resignation as delegate to all international conferences. On 7 May 1921 he refused to continue as Poland's representative to the League of Nations.

Paderewski's anger and disappointment was focused on Piłsudski, whom he accused of adventurism. He felt that for the sake of consolidating Polish control over the Eastern borders, to which Poland had a dubious claim, by entering into conflicts with the Ukrainian community which then led to a direct confrontation with the Soviet Union, and by conducting a badly thought-out policy towards the Lithuanians, the new Polish state had forfeited the goodwill of the European Powers. This he believed had led directly to their seeing Poland as a source of instability and conflict. Paderewski thus believed that the Teschen region had been lost to Czechoslovakia and Upper Silesia to Germany because of the Great Powers' vindictive attitude towards Poland after the conflict in the Ukraine. By linking the issue of rights in the Free City of Danzig to Polish willingness to accept Western mediation with the Soviet Union, Britain and France confirmed Paderewski's worst suspicions about their real motives.

In his memoirs Paderewski indicated that in retrospect he felt that his willingness to act as Poland's representative to the Conference of Ambassadors was a mistake. At the time, he distanced himself from the episode, merely stating that he suspected that he had been used by the government. Paderewski still thought, however, that he could play a role in Polish politics, that of saving the country from Piłsudski. During 1922, in the run-up to the presidential elections, several prominent politicians from the National Christian Movement approached him hoping that he would agree to stand. Their efforts came to nothing as there was little evidence of wider support for his candidacy. It was later said that Paderewski was only marginally interested in the possibility of becoming President, but that his wife was very keen and indeed that she felt particularly affronted when nothing came of the talks.

Paderewski's financial situation was perilous and his first task, on resigning all political and diplomatic responsibilities, was to restore it. He needed to earn money and playing the piano was the only way to do this. In May 1922, while on holiday in the United States, he sat at the piano after years of neglecting the instrument. After six weeks of strenuous practice he felt that he had regained his earlier proficiency and prepared a programme. His first concert and those which followed were sell-outs. The first took place on 22 November 1922 at Carnegie Hall in New York. Paderewski found out that *some people from within the musical circles forecast a total disaster. One particularly influential music critic in New York ... most earnestly forecast that the first recital would be a failure. He went so far as to take bets, that this would happen.*[3] As it turned out Paderewski astounded the critics with the quality of his playing. He and his listeners agreed that there was a maturity there which had been absent before. But still, even though the critics agreed that Paderewski showed a mastery of his instrument, there were those who wondered why during the years that followed he still attracted huge audiences to his concerts. The quality of his playing might well have improved and he was pleased with his performances, but there was the added attraction of the pianist being a world-famous personality, a legend in his own lifetime. Could it be that it was this, rather than his mastery of the keyboard, which led to his concerts selling-out? Whatever it was, Paderewski was entirely happy with his progress, first through the United States, then Europe and Australia. The takings were enormous and once more he felt financially secure. Most importantly, he was able to pay off his creditors.

> 'I felt that never had I heard such depth of expression, such richness of phrasing, or such insight into the whole world of music.'
>
> FULLER MAITLAND ON PADEREWSKI, NOVEMBER 1922[4]

It is interesting to speculate why a 62-year-old man continued to put himself through the hardship of touring when the financial pressures must have eased after the first few years. The only answer to that question is Paderewski's vanity. He had become accustomed to acclaim and admiration. His involvement in the Paris Peace Conference undoubtedly acted as a catalyst for his sense of self-importance, if not for his feeling that he was chosen by destiny to play a vital role in the restoration of Poland. Thus his artistic and musical talent, which he had ultimately used to further the Polish cause, led him in 1919 to the point where he no longer distinguished between the two roles. When he withdrew from the political arena, he was no longer lionised, and he missed the opportunity to influence the great men of the world. He must have felt that life had become boring and perhaps devoid of purpose. During his ten years of touring after 1922 he once more met politicians and the crowned heads of Europe. Again he was treated as a statesman and as a man of destiny. It is not difficult to understand why he clung to that role and indeed found it easy to believe that he was no less than what his audience and admirers wanted him to be.

For all the appearance of having left Poland behind and of concentrating on his musical activities, Paderewski continued to support Polish causes. This took the form of generous donations to institutions caring for war orphans and veterans. He was acutely aware of the hardship faced by the families of those who had been killed during the war. It was a well known fact that Paderewski could be easily persuaded to part with the proceeds of his concerts for any charitable institution dedicated to helping Poles. When in the United States he supported Polish émigré organisations and the Polish Catholic parishes there.[5] The latter cause was particularly close to his heart. The Polish community insisted on having Polish priests, something which the American Catholic Church, dominated by Irish priests, was not initially willing to allow, but in the end, afraid that the Polish community might establish its own church, the Vatican allowed the Poles to have their own priests.

In Poland the political crisis had deepened. News of the May 1926 coup reached Paderewski at home in Switzerland where he was preparing for a forthcoming tour of Australia. So shocking was the news that for several days he shut himself off from the world, refusing to communicate with anybody. He was particularly distressed by reports of fratricidal fighting and of the casualties in Warsaw. For Paderewski the coup was a personal affront as he had fought so hard to persuade world statesmen that Poland would be a force for stability in the region. Piłsudski's actions smacked of personality-driven politics and confirmed Westerners' worst suspicions about Poland not being ready for independence.

In years to come, while Paderewski cut himself off from any direct involvement in Polish politics, he remained in contact with a group of officers opposed to Piłsudski. By 1928 General Sikorski, one of Piłsudski's strongest opponents in the army, was communicating with Paderewski on a regular basis, providing him with information about the fate of the opposition and the increasing threat to democratic institutions. From him Paderewski found out about the imprisonment of officers who had opposed the coup and refused to participate in it. They had been imprisoned for remaining loyal to their oath and then dismissed from the army. During the years which followed, Sikorski sent Paderewski regular updates on how the regime progressively militarised all ministries, restricted civil rights and attacked national minorities and the opposition parties.

The Peasant Party also looked to Paderewski as a possible leader of the opposition, though it is doubtful that he ever seriously considered returning to active politics in Poland. Witos, for one, was convinced that Paderewski was the only person who had enough authority to oppose Piłsudski.[6] One of the prominent Poles who contacted him during the years of the Piłsudski regime was General Haller, who had commanded the Polish army raised in France during the First World War. The role of the Polish armed forces was one of the issues with which Paderewski had been closely concerned during the Paris Conference, and Haller came to see Paderewski as an ally. During the difficult years after his criticism of Piłsudski's coup he once more looked to Paderewski for support. Paderewski could in reality do little to help the Poles, other than to offer them financial support and give hospitality to those who made it into exile. Some of those who did were opposition politicians who had been imprisoned in the Brześć fortress in 1930.

In the late 1920s Paderewski started to think about the next generation of pianists. It was generally known that he did not like teaching, but in 1928 he gathered a group of young Polish pianists at his Swiss residence for summer courses. Unfortunately most of the participants turned out to have insufficient talent and staying power to establish themselves in the European musical community. The exception was Witold Małcużyński, who studied with him for a short time.[8] The public viewed Paderewski as an outstanding musician but younger performers and composers did not rate him highly. His repertoire remained unchanged over the years, with a distinct preference for Chopin and Liszt, and the odd piece by Johann Sebastian Bach. He responded to criticism of his failure to play works by younger composers by stating that he did not feel that they were composing for the piano but for orchestras. It has been suggested that his lack of interest in more up-to-date compositions stemmed from the fact that once he gave up composing he lost the feel for works which required a more profound understanding of the relationship between the piano and an orchestra. On occasions he was heard making positive comments about Igor Stravinsky and Claude Debussy, but he did not have a feel for their music and did not play it. As a frequent visitor to the United States he heard jazz, but he dismissed the players as *the Bolsheviks of*

> 'The wrong that has been done to you is a wrong done to the whole nation, since it has undermined faith in the administration of justice in Poland.'
> PADEREWSKI TO AN OPPOSITION POLITICIAN IMPRISONED BY THE PIŁSUDSKI REGIME.[7]

*music.*[9] Perhaps Paderewski was simply too old to learn new forms of expression and to understand new music. Although polite about new music, he remained committed to Chopin and Liszt.

The Great Depression hit the Polish community in the United States particularly badly as Poles were usually concentrated in unskilled jobs. It effectively destroyed all previous efforts made by their community leaders to improve the image of Poles in the United States. Earlier attempts to unify the different Polish organisations in order to create a stronger lobby had come to nothing. Paderewski had always shown a great interest in the Polish community's social and political activities and it had been his dream that Poles in the United States would be able to influence the government of the United States to pursue pro-Polish policies. He was therefore saddened to hear of their economic plight. But his concern and awareness of the human costs of the Depression extended beyond the Polish community. In 1932 he donated all proceeds from a concert at Madison Square Gardens to a fund for unemployed musicians. He made a similar gesture in 1933 when after a concert at the Albert Hall he made a sizeable contribution to a charity supporting musicians in London.

In January 1934 Helena Paderewska died. She had dedicated her life to taking care of everything so that her famous husband would have nothing to worry about and could focus on nurturing his great talent. As is frequently the case with wives of great men, she acted as the guardian of his time and custodian of his peace. Many perceived her to have had her own ambitions, in particular to becoming the wife of Poland's President. In reality he needed her to perform her protective role and gladly hid behind her in order to create the illusion that he was generous with his time and welcoming of visitors, while she was seen as the one restricting access to her husband. It was true that she never saw the distinction between his role as an artist and the brief period when he became Prime Minister. Yet her interference during that time, though inappropriate, is perhaps understandable. During the couple's brief period in Warsaw people mocked her dress sense and indifference to protocol. Paderewski refused to hear a word said against her and was personally deeply wounded when he heard of the fun made of her. To him she was both a surrogate mother and a loyal companion. There can be no doubt his peace of mind and ability to function as an artist depended on the tranquil and trouble-free environment that she created for him.

Helena also made her own contribution to helping Poland. She became known as an accomplished poultry breeder and funded the training of women from Poland in the most up to date breeding techniques. These were small steps, but in agriculturally-backward Poland, these gestures were important. In 1931 she had become increasingly frail, confused and forgetful. Paderewski refused to face up to the implications of her deterioration and he remained a loyal husband to the end. During the last years of her life she appeared unaware of the world around her. Her death reminded Paderewski of his own age and the passing of the generation to which he belonged. He faced the tragic fact that he had outlived his relatives and friends.

When Helena Paderewska died her husband fell into a deep depression and it was believed that he would give up playing. This did not happen. On the contrary, not only did he return to touring but surprisingly in 1937 he agreed to collaborate in the making of a film. In those days, the cinema was still viewed by the cultured classes as rather vulgar, smacking of popular entertainment. But Paderewski was persuaded to play an aging pianist, something which hardly taxed his acting skills. *Moonlight Sonata* was a box-office success and is the only surviving film of Paderewski playing the piano. He was reported to have enjoyed the experience.

Political activities also offered a distraction from his grief, sense of loss and old age. After Piłsudski's death in 1935 the opposition had high hopes that the regime would collapse or at least would be weakened. Paderewski became the focal point of hopes for a renewal. The 'Rule of the Colonels' however continued to maintain a grip on the political life in Poland and the opposition parties were not able to break its stranglehold. The other factor which played into the hands of the post-Piłsudski regime was disunity between the various opposition parties. In February 1936 Paderewski hosted a meeting of a number of opposition leaders in his house in Switzerland. Of these Wincenty Witos, General Haller and General Sikorski were the most prominent. The plan was to build a broadly-based front to oppose the military rulers. The group came to be known as the Front Morges, after the town where Paderewski lived. Unfortunately, in spite of the best of intentions none of the party leaders had enough authority or following in Poland to pose a threat to the regime. Paderewski, although as always an attentive host, seemed to be showing his age and was genuinely unable to offer any help other than acting as a patron of the movement.[10]

The growth of Nazi aggression saddened Paderewski immensely. He loathed Hitler and was horrified by news of anti-Semitic atrocities. In a gesture which bore the hallmarks of a need to reaffirm his previous assertions that he was not anti-Semitic, Paderewski declared that he would not play in any country which introduced legislation against its

Jewish community. During the critical months preceding the outbreak of the war he remained in touch with opposition leaders in Poland and followed the news avidly. Surprisingly, considering his earlier well-known disapproval of Piłsudski's policies of using military force to resolve territorial disputes with neighbouring states, he was delighted to hear that Poland had reclaimed disputed territories from Czechoslovakia in October 1938. The fact that this was done after Germany succeeded in obtaining French and British approval for the dismemberment of Czechoslovakia and had been coordinated with the Nazis was something he chose not to dwell on. Like many Poles, he succumbed to patriotic euphoria and was willing to forgive the military regime its recent policies when it was seen to be restoring Poland's dignity and even preparing to fight Germany.

When Germany attacked Poland on 1 September 1939 Paderewski was at home in Switzerland. There he also heard of the Soviet invasion of Eastern Poland on 18 September. On 24 August Nazi Germany and the Soviet Union had signed a Non-Aggression Pact, which came to be known as the Ribbentrop-Molotov Pact from the names of the two signatories. The secret annex of the pact outlined areas which both sides would take over after the outbreak of the German-Polish war. This agreement meant that once the Wehrmacht attacked Poland, the Soviet Union would benefit from Poland's defeat. The Polish government, unable to continue the fight against the two invaders, departed for Romania where, unexpectedly and on German instructions, it was interned. General Sikorski, with French assistance, managed to escape and went to Paris, visiting Paderewski on the way. Once in Paris, the battle to establish a government in exile was fought out between the army leaders who wanted to retain control over all political matters and the leaders of the opposition parties who had also arrived. Sikorski, supported by the opposition parties and backed by the French authorities, became the Prime Minister. The presidency was a more complex issue as the Polish president interned in Romania resigned and appointed a successor, Władysław Raczkiewicz, who allied himself with the military groups who saw themselves as preserving Piłsudski's legacy. Sikorski and the opposition parties initially wanted Paderewski to become President of the government in exile. After some reflection and undoubtedly due to Paderewski's rapidly deteriorating health this plan was abandoned. Nevertheless, out of respect he was consulted and included in all decisions. He, more than any other Polish leader outside occupied Poland, had the stature to bring together the squabbling Polish community. The aim was to determine how the fight to liberate Poland could be resumed.

Paderewski still thought of the fight for Poland in terms of what he had been able to achieve during the First World War. He wrote to his personal friends: to Mussolini, whom he upbraided for supporting German occupation of Poland; to Roosevelt whom he asked to reaffirm that Poland would be restored to the map of Europe; and to Mahatma Gandhi to make sure that he would not hinder Britain from making a commitment to fight for Poland. All responded, but nothing could be done to help Poland at that time. During the following months Paderewski had to consider his own position, in particular when Germany attacked France. Fortunately he was personally acquainted with General Pétain, the head of the Vichy government established in unoccupied France. In September 1940 Paderewski decided to leave for the United States. To reach the coast he had to cross France and then proceed to Spain and Portugal to catch a ship. The German authorities who could count on the two governments' compliance with any request that would be made to them, gave the impression of wanting to detain him in Europe, but diplomatic pressure was put on Spain and Portugal to allow him to proceed. President Roosevelt had let General Franco know that he expected Paderewski to be treated with respect. Such a message could not be ignored even if the German government would have wanted him kept in Spain. Paderewski arrived in the United States on 6 November 1940.

Once there, Paderewski threw himself into a routine which he knew only too well, of lecturing, speaking at public events and hosting fund-raising activities. His view was that the United States should be persuaded to actively support the British government in its pursuit of the war. *What sacrifice have you really made to help the Allied Democracies resist the barbarous aggression?*[11] was the question he asked of his audiences. On 21 June 1941 he died, having earlier collapsed during a public event in support of the war effort. One of the most fitting phrases describing Paderewski was uttered by Gabriel Hanotaux who declared 'this Pole will come to be judged by history not only as one of the greatest representatives of his nation, but also of his century'.[12]

# Conclusion

History has been kind to Paderewski and Dmowski. Whereas during the inter-war period the public and politicians believed that they had been responsible for the unfavourable conditions imposed on Poland at the Paris Peace Conference, this opinion did not endure. The events of the Second World War brought a new perspective and a deeper understanding of the degree to which Poland was and still is dependent on international support. This means that it is their long term commitment to fighting for the restoration of Poland rather than just their negotiations in Paris that are appreciated.

Not surprisingly, Paderewski's political activities have been largely forgotten and he is remembered as Poland's cultural ambassador. Dmowski, however, still evokes fierce loyalty and deep hostility in equal measure. He is remembered for his nationalist theories and for his anti-Semitism. The right wing has always been divided between those who consider Dmowski to be the true father of the Polish nationalist movement and those who see Piłsudski as the man who through his deeds made Poland's restoration possible. To the latter his disregard for democracy and bullish attitude towards the Great Powers is seen as a sign of strength.

At the Paris Peace Conference the Polish case was not the most important one, a point which is often not appreciated by the Poles themselves. During the Conference Poland's fate was always viewed in terms of the German question and later also that of Bolshevik Russia. Thus efforts made by the two Poles in Paris were rarely appreciated for what they were and instead Polish tactics were seen as creating problems. While the British, French, Italian and American leaders set the pace, the discussions on the actual details of territorial adjustments were driven by points made by Dmowski and Paderewski. It is they who presented documents and made submissions which fleshed out what had been only general points. But it is for those reasons that the contribution made by the two formidable Poles tends to be minimised if not outright ignored.

The borders within which the new Polish state was established after the First World War were the cause of constant conflict between Poland and its neighbours the Soviet Union, Czechoslovakia and Germany. Although the Polish-German border was, with the exception of Upper Silesia where the uprisings caused a revision of decisions made earlier, defined at the Paris Conference, neither state felt that it had been a just one. Poland felt particularly aggrieved that it was not granted Danzig. Germany, on the other hand, resented the loss of the Poznań region and later of Upper Silesia. Relations between Poland and Germany were strained throughout the inter-war period, even before the Nazis came to power with the explicit aim of overthrowing the Versailles Treaty. It is therefore surprising that Czechoslovakia and not Poland was the first object of Nazi aggression. It was not until October 1938 that Ribbentrop demanded that Poland make concessions in the Corridor by the granting of an extraterritorial link between the Free City of Danzig and East Prussia. This the Poles rejected, signalling that they would fight if Germany tried to revise the post-war borders. Poland's fate was thus sealed when from January 1939 German propaganda increasingly portrayed Poland as oppressing its German community. In the meantime Nazi organisations started financing Ukrainian paramilitary groups in Slovakia and Poland, hoping to benefit from the extremely bad relations between the Polish state and its Ukrainian community. On 1 September 1939 Nazi Germany unleashed a military onslaught on Poland. By 18 September Poland's fate was sealed when the Red Army occupied over one-third of Polish territory in the East.

The issue of Teschen remained a bone of contention between Poland and Czechoslovakia throughout the interwar period, but it was not the only issue which plagued relations between the two states. The Poles felt that Czechoslovakia had been favoured by France. Relations between the two states were always strained and never more so than when in February 1938 Hitler decided to take up the cause of the German community in Czechoslovakia which he portrayed as being victims of mistreatment. His real aim was the destruction of the despised Czechoslovak state. Poland and Hungary, the two states which had lost territories to Czechoslovakia in 1919, allied themselves with Germany. When at the Munich Conference in September 1938, Germany, Italy, France and Britain put pressure on Czechoslovakia to accept the secession of areas inhabited by its German minority, Poland activated its plans to regain territories which it had claimed in 1919. This lack of unity between the two potential victims of Nazi aggression had its roots in the conflicts over the Teschen region and ultimately made it possible for Germany to destroy first Czechoslovakia and then Poland.

The issue of Wilno which had been the bone of contention

between Lithuania and Poland and which Poland took despite international disapproval likewise affected Polish-Lithuanian relations throughout the inter-war period. Although Lithuania was anxious about increasing German influence on the Baltic coast, it was more fearful of Poland and resisted all Polish attempts to establish itself as a potential protector of the region against Germany and the Soviet Union.

To the new Polish state the Soviet Union remained a constant source of anxiety. The precarious military victory when the Red Army was defeated in Poland acted as a warning. Military plans developed during the inter-war period assumed that the Soviet Union was the most likely aggressor. Soviet power was perceived to be twofold: on the one hand this was a state determined to review the border settlements reached at the Riga Conference, and on the other hand, it was a political force which could try to destroy Polish independence by imposing a communist regime.

The way in which Poland's borders in the East were defined, namely through a series of military campaigns frequently facing local resistance, as was the case in Eastern Galicia and in the Belorussian areas, had an impact on the Polish state's relations with its minority communities. After denying these communities the right to self-determination and having forcibly incorporated them within its border, they were a source of internal instability, threatening to ally themselves with Poland's enemies and seeking to benefit from a time of weakness, as proved to be the case with the Ukrainians. All these factors came into play when Poland faced the threat of German aggression and each contributed, albeit not decisively, to Poland's defeat.

On the international stage the legacy of the way in which the two Polish delegates negotiated in Paris, and Piłsudski's arrogance in continuing with military action in spite of explicit requests not to, was considerable. The French government came to see Poland as an unreliable partner in the East while successive British governments had no desire to intervene in the Polish-German conflict, in particular when in the autumn of 1938 it looked as if the Germans might attempt to take Danzig. It was therefore an unusual reversal of Britain's policy when in March 1939 Chamberlain's government offered a guarantee of Polish security; in fact this was more a reflection of a deeper anxiety about Germany's growing influence in the East rather than any genuine wish to protect Poland.

Throughout the Second World War, in spite of a formidable contribution to the Allied war effort by the Polish government-in-exile, Britain was not prepared to challenge the Soviet Union by demanding a commitment to the return of the territories taken in September 1939. While Britain's military dependence on the Soviet Union clearly was the main cause of this timorousness, there was little sympathy for the restoration of an Eastern border beyond the ethnic boundary of the Curzon Line, which had been favoured by Britain in 1920. Poland's borders after the Second World War, with the exception of the Polish-German border, were defined as a result of Soviet policies. Polish politicians in exile had no influence over these matters, though they did try, unsuccessfully, to obtain British support for the restoration of the pre-war borders. The wartime allies agreed that Poland should benefit from Germany's defeat and the border was set on the two rivers, the Oder and its tributary the Neisse. East and West Prussia, including Danzig, were incorporated into Poland and the German inhabitants of those areas were forcibly removed. The frontiers of the Polish state were moved dramatically to the West. After the Second World War Poland became a nation state. The Jewish community had been effectively wiped out by the Nazis, while the majority of non-Polish areas had been incorporated into the Soviet Union.

The turbulent events of 1919–20, when the borders of the restored state were defined, still had their implications on the period immediately after the Second World War. Eastern Galicia was divided between Poland and the Soviet Union. The Ukrainian community resisted until in 1947 it was forcefully uprooted and moved to the newly-acquired territories in Western Poland. The Polish Communist government, in a manner not much different from the policies pursued by successive governments during the inter-war period, made it impossible for the Ukrainians to practice their faith, to develop their culture or to speak their language. Thus the policy of denial of the Ukrainian right to self-determination continued. Only after the fall of Communism and the disintegration of the Soviet Union did an independent Ukraine and Belorussia emerge.

# Notes

## 1 Ignacy Paderewski

1. Ignacy Jan Paderewski and Mary Lawton, *The Paderewski Memoirs* (Collins, London: 1939) p 23, hereafter *The Paderewski Memoirs*.
2. *The Paderewski Memoirs*, p 36.
3. R Wapiński, *Ignacy Paderewski* (Zakład im, Ossolińskich, Wrocław: 1999) p 20.
4. H Opieński, *Ignacy Paderewski* (Warszawa: 1960) pp 24–5.
5. Wapiński, *Ignacy Paderewski*, pp 32–4.
6. A Zamoyski, *Paderewski* (Collins, London: 1982) pp 54–5.
7. *The Paderewski Memoirs*, p 240.
8. Wapiński, *Ignacy Paderewski*, pp 32–3.
9. *The Paderewski Memoirs*, p 184.
10. *The Paderewski Memoirs*, p 364.
11. Zamoyski, *Paderewski*, p 129.
12. Marian Marek Drozdowski, *Ignacy Jan Paderewski. A Political Biography* (Interpress, Kraków: 1981) p 33.
13. *The Paderewski Memoirs*, pp 379–81.

14. *The Paderewski Memoirs*, pp 379–81.
15. *The Paderewski Memoirs*, pp 384–5.

## 2 Roman Dmowski

1. Alvin Marcus Fountain II, *Roman Dmowski: Party, Tactics, Ideology 1895–1907* (East European Monographs, Boulder, Col: 1980) p 8.
2. Roman Dmowski. *Myśl Nowoczesnego Polaka* (Młode Stronnictwo Narodowe. Lonayn: 1953) p 27.
3. Krzysztof Kowalec, *Roman Dmowski* (Editions Spotkania, Warszawa: 1996) p 10.
4. Andrzej Micewski, *Roman Dmowski* (Wydawnictwo 'Verum', Warszawa: 1971) p 24.
5. Micewski, *Roman Dmowski*, pp 28–31.
6. Mariusz Kułakowski, *Roman Dmowski w świetle listów i wspomnień*, Vol I (Gryf Publications Ltd, London: 1968) p 144.
7. Kułakowski, *Roman Dmowski w świetle listów I wspomnień*, Vol I, p 144.
8. Fountain, *Roman Dmowski: Party, Tactics, Ideology 1895–1907*, p 30.
9. Fountain, *Roman Dmowski: Party, Tactics, Ideology 1895–1907*, pp 41–2.
10. Roman Dmowski, *Myśl Nowoczesnego Polaka*, first serialised in 1902.
11. Fountain, *Roman Dmowski: Party, Tactics, Ideology 1895–1907*, p 43.
12. Dmowski, *Myśl Nowoczesnego Polaka*, p 56.
13. Dmowski, *Myśl Nowoczesnego Polaka*, p 103.
14. Dmowski, *Myśl Nowoczesnego Polaka*, 7th Edition, p 91.
15. Kowalec, *Roman Dmowski*, pp 116–21.

## 3 The First World War

1. Wiktor Sukiennicki, *East Central Europe During World War I: From Foreign Domination to National Independence* (East European Monographs, Boulder, Col: 1984) p 92.

2. Endone Andrzej Garlicki, *Józef Piłsudski. 1867–1935* (Czytelnik, Warszawa: 1988) p 143.

3. Sukiennicki, *East Central Europe During World War I*, p 266.

4. Titus Komarnicki, *Rebirth of the Polish Republic. A Study in the Diplomatic History of Europe, 1914–1920* (William Heinemann Ltd, London: 1957) pp 93–7.

5. Andrzej Garlicki, *Józef Piłsudski 1867–1935* (Scholar Press, Aldershot: 1995) pp 86–7.

6. Komarnicki, *Rebirth of the Polish Republic*, p 30.

7. *The Paderewski Memoirs*, pp 389–90.

8. *The Paderewski Memoirs*, p 389.

9. Ignacy Jan Paderewski and Mary Lawton, *Pamiętniki, 1912–1932* (Polskie Wydawnictwo Muzyczne, Warszawa: 1992) p 27.

10. Drozdowski, *Ignacy Jan Paderewski*, p 75.

11. Paderewski and Lawton, *Pamiętniki, 1912–1932*, p 37.

12. Zamoyski, *Paderewski*, p 156.

13. Wapiński, *Ignacy Paderewski*, pp 77–8.

14. Drozdowski, *Ignacy Jan Paderewski*, p 91.

15. Paul Latawski, 'Roman Dmowski, the Polish Question, and the Western Opinion, 1915–18: The Case of Britain' in Paul Latawski (ed), *The Reconstruction of Poland, 1914–21* (Macmillan, Houndmills: 1992) p 3.

16. Latawski, 'Roman Dmowski, the Polish Question, and the Western Opinion, 1915–18: The Case of Britain', p 8.

17. Latawski, 'Roman Dmowski, the Polish Question, and the Western Opinion, 1915–18: The Case of Britain', pp 6–7.

18. Roman Dmowski, *Polityka Polska i Odbudowanie Państwa*, Vol II (Hanower: 1947) p 37.

19. Georges Clemenceau, *Grandeur and Misery of Victory* (G G Harrap, London: 1930) p 180.

## 4 The Emergence of Independent Poland

1. Kay Lundgreen-Nielsen, *The Polish Problem at the Paris Peace Conference. A Study of the Policies of the Great Powers and the Poles, 1918–1919* (Odense University Press, Odense: 1979) p 35.

2. Kowalec, *Roman Dmowski*, pp 195–8.

3. Garlicki, *Józef Piłsudski*, p 88.

4. Kowalec, *Roman Dmowski*, pp 192–4.

5. Jan Zamoyski, *Powrót na mapę. Polski Komitet Narodowy w Paryżu 1914–1919* (Państwowe Wydawnictwo Naukowe, Warszawa: 1991) pp 70–2.

6. Paderewski and Lawton, *Pamiętniki, 1912–1932*, p 55.

7. Komarnicki, *Rebirth of the Polish Republic*, p 231.

8. Kowalec, *Roman Dmowski*, p 206.

9. Drozdowski, *Ignacy Jan Paderewski*, pp 135–6.

10. Paderewski and Lawton, *Pamiętniki, 1912–1932*, p 58.

11. Paderewski and Lawton, *Pamiętniki, 1912–1932*, p 58.

12. Wapiński, *Ignacy Paderewski*, p 262.

13. Zamoyski, *Paderewski*, p 170.

14. Paderewski and Lawton, *Pamiętniki, 1912–1932*, p 63.

15. Wapiński, *Ignacy Paderewski*, p 98.

16. Paderewski and Lawton, *Pamiętniki, 1912–1932*, p 70.

17. Paderewski and Lawton, *Pamiętniki, 1912–1932*, p 74.

## 5 Paris

1. F S Marston, *The Peace Conference of 1919. Organisation and Procedure* (Oxford University Press, London: 1944) p 111.

2. Lundgreen-Neilsen, *The Polish Problem at the Paris Peace Conference*, pp 177–8.

3. Harold Nicolson, *Peacemakers 1919* (Constable and Co Ltd, London: 1933) p 1.

4. Marston, *The Peace Conference of 1919*, pp 106–7.

5. Margaret Macmillan, *Peacemakers. The Paris Conference of 1919 and Its Attempt to End War* (John Murray, London: 2001) pp 227–8.

6. Marston, *The Peace Conference of 1919*, p 124.

7. J Pajewski (ed), *Problem Polsko-Niemiecki w Traktacie Wesalskim* (Instytut Zachodni, Poznań: 1963) pp pp 219–28.

8. Lundgreen-Neilsen, *The Polish Problem at the Paris Peace Conference*, pp 98–102.

9. Mariusz Kułakowski, *Roman Dmowski w świetle listów i wspomnień*, Vol II (Gryf Publications Ltd, London: 1972) p 147.

10. Dmowski, *Polityka Polska i Odbudowanie Państwa*, Vol II, p 166.

11. David Lloyd George, *The Truth about the Peace Treaties*, Vol I (Victor Gollancz Ltd, London: 1938) pp 308–12.

12. Lloyd George, *The Truth about the Peace Treaties*, Vol I, p 313.

13. Lloyd George, *The Truth about the Peace Treaties*, Vol I, pp 313–14.

14. Dmowski, *Polityka Polska i Odbudowanie Państwa*, Vol II, p 161.

15. Zamoyski, *Paderewski*, pp 186–7.

16. Kułakowski, *Roman Dmowski w świetle listów i wspomnień*, Vol II, pp 152–3.

17. Kułakowski, *Roman Dmowski w świetle listów i wspomnień*, Vol II, p 158.

18. Kułakowski, *Roman Dmowski w świetle listów i wspomnień*, Vol II, p 159.

19. Roman Wapiński, *Roman Dmowski* (Wydawnictwo Lubelskie, Lublin: 1988) pp 281–2.

20. Wapiński, *Roman Dmowski*, p 286.

21. Zamoyski, *Paderewski*, pp 196–9.

22. Anna M Cienciała, 'The Battle for Danzig and the Polish Corridor at the Paris Peace Conference of 1919' in Paul Latawski (ed), *The Reconstruction of Poland, 1914–21* (Macmillan, Houndmills: 1992) pp 81–4.

23. Zamoyski, *Paderewski*, pp 186–8.

24. Anna M Cienciała and Titus Komarnicki, *From Versailles to Locarno, Keys to Polish Foreign Policy 1919–1925* (Lawrence, Kansas University Press: 1984) p 156.

25. Kułakowski, *Roman Dmowski w świetle listów i wspomnień*, Vol II, pp 170–1.

26. Lundgreen-Neilsen, *The Polish Problem at the Paris Peace Conference*, pp 291–4.

27. Lundgreen-Neilsen, *The Polish Problem at the Paris Peace Conference*, pp 288–91.

28. Lundgreen-Neilsen, *The Polish Problem at the Paris Peace Conference*, pp 302–7.

29. J M Keynes, *The Economic Consequences of the Peace* (Macmillan and Co, Ltd, London: 1920) p 273.

## 6 Unfinished Business

1. Paderewski and Lawton, *Pamiętniki,1912–1923*, p 73.
2. Zamoyski, *Paderewski*, pp 201–2.
3. Zamoyski, *Paderewski*, pp 202–3.
4. Drozdowski, *Ignacy Jan Paderewski*, pp 166–70.
5. Zamoyski, *Paderewski*, p 205.
6. Drozdowski, *Ignacy Jan Paderewski*, p 167.
7. Wapiński, *Ignacy Paderewski*, p 152.
8. Wapiński, *Ignacy Paderewski*, pp 157–8.
9. Cienciała and Komarnicki, *From Versailles to Locarno*, pp 46–50.
10. Cienciała and Komarnicki, *From Versailles to Locarno*, pp 60–1.
11. Cienciała and Komarnicki, *From Versailles to Locarno*, pp 88–90.
12. Garlicki, *Józef Piłsudski, 1867–1935*, pp 93–101.
13. Norman Davies, *White Eagle, Red Star. The Polish-Soviet War, 1919–1920* (Macdonald, London: 1972) pp 188–225.

## 7 The Realities of Independent Poland

1. Wapiński, *Roman Dmowski*, pp 290–1.
2. Kowalec, *Roman Dmowski*, p 244.
3. Wapiński, *Roman Dmowski*, p 247.
4. Wapiński, *Roman Dmowski*, p 296.
5. Kułakowski, *Roman Dmowski w świetle listów i wspomnień*, Vol II, p 219.
6. Kułakowski, *Roman Dmowski w świetle listów i wspomnień*, Vol II, pp 219–20.
7. Kowalec, *Roman Dmowski*, pp 274–7.
8. Garlicki, *Józef Piłsudski*, p 138.
9. Kowalec. *Roman Dmowski*, pp 283–5.

10. Micewski, *Roman Dmowski*, p 323.
11. Kowalec. *Roman Dmowski*, pp 282–5.
12. Wapiński, *Roman Dmowski*, pp 351–2.
13. Wapiński, *Roman Dmowski*, p 377.
14. Micewski, *Roman Dmowski*, p 401.

## 8 The Return to the Piano

1. Paderewski and Lawton, *Pamiętniki 1912–1932*, p 77.
2. Wapiński, *Ignacy Paderewski*, p 158.
3. Paderewski and Lawton, *Pamiętniki 1912–1932*, p 80.
4. Zamoyski, *Paderewski*, p 217.
5. Drozdowski, *Ignacy Jan Paderewski*, pp 181–2.
6. Wapiński, *Ignacy Paderewski*, p 184.
7. Wapiński, *Ignacy Paderewski*, p 185.
8. Zamoyski, *Paderewski*, pp 221–2.
9. Zamoyski, *Paderewski*, p 221.
10. Drozdowski, *Ignacy Jan Paderwski*, pp 204–5.
11. Zamoyski, *Paderewski*, p 236.
12. Zamoyski, *Paderewski*, p 239.

# Chronology

| YEAR | AGE | THE LIFE AND THE LAND |
|------|-----|----------------------|
| **1860** | | 6 Nov: Ignacy Paderewski (IP) born. His mother dies a few days later. |
| **1863** | 3 | January Uprising; IP's father arrested by Russian authorities on suspicion of having aided the insurrectionists. |
| **1864** | 4 | 9 Aug: Roman Dmowski born. |
| **1872** | 12 | IP enrolls at the Music Institute in Warsaw. |
| **1878** | 18 | IP graduates from Warsaw Music Institute. |
| **1880** | 20 | 7 Jan: IP marries Antonina Korsakówna. 18 Oct: IP's only child Alfred born; Antonina dies 10 days later. |
| **1882** | 22 | January: IP to Berlin to study the piano. |
| **1884** | 24 | IP goes to Vienna; piano lessons with Theodor Leschitzkey. |
| **1885** | 25 | IP employed at the Strasbourg Conservatoire. |
| **1888** | 26 | IP gives first concerts in Paris. |

| YEAR | HISTORY | CULTURE |
|------|---------|---------|
| 1860 | Garibaldi lands in Italy. Abraham Lincoln elected US President. | Wilkie Collins, *The Woman in White*. |
| 1863 | American Civil War: Confederate defeats at Gettysburg and Vicksburg. | Charles Kingsley, *The Water Babies*. |
| 1864 | Schleswig War: Austrian and Prussian troops defeat Danes. | Tolstoy, *War and Peace* (–1869). |
| 1872 | Three Emperors' League (Germany, Russia, Austria-Hungary) established in Berlin. | Turgenev, *A Month in the Country*. |
| 1878 | Russo-Turkish War ends. | Ruskin-Whistler libel case. |
| 1880 | France annexes Tahiti. Transvaal Republic declares independence from Britain. | Dostoevsky, *The Brothers Karamazov*. |
| 1882 | Triple Alliance between Italy, Germany and Austria-Hungary. | Tchaikovsky, '1812 Overture'. |
| 1884 | Germans occupy South-West Africa. Gold discovered in the Transvaal. | Mark Twain, *Huckleberry Finn*. |
| 1885 | General Gordon killed in fall of Khartoum to the Mahdi. | Gilbert and Sullivan, operetta 'The Mikado'. |
| 1888 | Kaiser Wilhelm II accedes to the throne. | Rudyard Kipling, *Plain Tales from the Hills*. |

| YEAR | AGE | THE LIFE AND THE LAND |
|------|-----|------------------------|
| 1889 | 29 | IP tours Belgium, the Netherlands, Germany, Hungary and Poland; settles in Paris and brings son to join him. |
| 1890 | 30 | IP tours Britain receiving negative reviews. |
| 1891 | 31 | Jun: IP's second tour of London.<br><br>11 Nov: IP arrives in the USA. |
| 1892 | 32 | Nov: IP's second tour of the USA. |
| 1895 | 35 | IP's third tour of the USA.<br>Dmowski begins writing for nationalist newspapers in Lwów. |
| 1899 | 39 | 31 May: IP marries Helena Górska; purchases Villa Rion-Bosson in Switzerland. |
| 1900 | 40 | Jun: IP's son Alfred dies. |
| 1901 | 41 | IP completes his only opera, *Manru*. |
| 1902 | | Dmowski outlines the main tenets of his ideology in a series of articles later published as *The Thoughts of a Modern Pole*. |
| 1904 | 34 | Jan: IP performs before Tsar Nicholas II; later tours Australia and New Zealand.<br>Dmowski and Piłsudski in Toyko to seek support for Polish independence. |

| YEAR | HISTORY | CULTURE |
| --- | --- | --- |
| 1889 | Austro-Hungarian Crown Prince Rudolf commits suicide at Mayerling.<br>London Dock Strike. | Jerome K Jerome, *Three Men in a Boat*.<br>Richard Strauss, symphonic poem 'Don Juan'. |
| 1890 | Bismarck dismissed by Wilhelm II. | Oscar Wilde, *The Picture of Dorian Gray*. |
| 1891 | Triple Alliance (Austria-Hungary, Germany, Italy) renewed for 12 years.<br>Franco-Russian entente. | Thomas Hardy, *Tess of the D'Urbervilles*. |
| 1892 | Pan-Slav Conference in Krakow. | Israel Zangwill, *Children of the Ghetto*. |
| 1895 | Sino-Japanese War ends.<br>Jameson Raid into Transvaal. | H G Wells, *The Time Machine*. |
| 1899 | Outbreak of Second Boer War.<br>First Peace Conference at the Hague. | Pinero, *Trelawny of the Wells*.<br>Elgar, 'Enigma Variations'. |
| 1900 | Boxer Rising in China. | Joseph Conrad, *Lord Jim*. |
| 1901 | Death of Queen Victoria. | Strindberg, *Dances of Death*. |
| 1902 | Treaty of Vereenigung ends Boer War<br>Triple Alliance between Austria, Germany and Italy renewed for another six years. | Maxim Gorki, *Lower Depths*.<br>Elgar, 'Pomp and Circumstance March No 1'. |
| 1904 | Entente Cordiale settles British-French colonial differences.<br>Outbreak of Russo-Japanese War. | J M Barrie, *Peter Pan*.<br>Anton Chekhov, *The Cherry Orchard*. |

| YEAR | AGE | THE LIFE AND THE LAND |
|------|-----|------------------------|
| **1905** | 41 | 27 Jan: General strike in Polish areas under Russian control. |
| | | 30 Oct: Tsarist manifesto promising liberal reforms and elections to a Duma |
| | | Nov: Martial law in Russian-controlled Poland. |
| **1911** | 51 | IP tours South America. |
| **1913** | 53 | IP tours USA; attacked for alleged anti-Semitism for financing Dmowski. |
| **1914** | 54 | 5 Feb: IP issues formal statement denying anti-Semitism. |
| | | 14 Aug: Proclamation to the Poles by Grand Duke Nicholas. |
| | | 26–30 Aug: Russian Second Army defeated at Battle of Tannenberg. |
| | | Sep: Russian First Army defeated at First Battle of Masurian Lakes. |
| **1915** | 55 | 22 Jan: IP helps establish General Commission for Polish Relief in Switzerland. |
| | | Feb: Russians defeated at Second Battle of Masurian Lakes. |
| | | Mar: IP visits Britain to secure support for the Commission for Polish Relief. |
| | | 15 Apr: IP arrives in USA. |
| | | May: Russians defeated by Austrians in Galicia. |
| | | 5 Aug: Germans occupy Warsaw. |

| YEAR | HISTORY | CULTURE |
|------|---------|---------|
| 1905 | Anglo-Japanese alliance renewed for ten years. | E M Forster, *Where Angels Fear to Tread*. |
|      | Albert Einstein develops his Special Theory of Relativity. | Edith Wharton, *House of Mirth*. |
| 1911 | Russian Premier Stolypin assassinated. | Strauss, 'Der Rosenkavalier'. |
| 1913 | Second Balkan war breaks out. | Thomas Mann, *Death in Venice*. |
| 1914 | Archduke Franz Ferdinand of Austria-Hungary and his wife are assassinated in Sarajevo. | James Joyce, *Dubliners*. |
|      | Outbreak of First World War: Battles of Mons, the Marne and First Ypres: trench warfare on the Western Front. | Film: Charlie Chaplin in *Making a Living*. |
| 1915 | First World War: Battles of Neuve Chapelle and Loos. The 'Shells Scandal'. | Joseph Conrad, *Victory*. |
|      | Gallipoli campaign. | John Buchan, *The Thirty-Nine Steps*. |
|      | Germans sink the British liner *Lusitania*, killing 1,198. | Ezra Pound, *Cathay*. |
|      | Germans execute British nurse Edith Cavell in Brussels for harbouring British prisoners. | Film: *The Birth of a Nation*. |

| YEAR | AGE | THE LIFE AND THE LAND |
|------|-----|----------------------|
| **1916** | 56 | 6 Nov: Post-war revival of autonomous Poland promised by German and Austrian Emperors; US President Wilson promises IP resurrection of Poland. |
| | | 26 Dec: Germans form Provisional Council of State in occupied Polish territories. |
| **1917** | 57 | 22 Jan: Wilson's declaration to Senate on Polish Question. |
| | | Feb: Revolution in Russia; abdication of Tsar and establishment of the dual authority of the Provisional Government and the Petrograd Soviet. |
| | | 21 Jul: Piłsudski arrested by Austrian authorities. |
| | | 15 Aug: Polish National Committee (KNP) formed in Lausanne. |
| | | Sep: Germans form Regency Council in occupied Polish territories. |
| | | 20 Nov: Ukrainian Central Council proclaims Ukrainian Peoples' Republic in Kiev. |

| YEAR | HISTORY | CULTURE |
|------|---------|---------|
| 1916 | First World War: | Lionel Curtis, *The Commonwealth of Nations.* |
| | Western Front: | James Joyce, *Portrait of an Artist as a Young Man.* |
| | Battle of Verdun, Battle of the Somme. | |
| | The Battle of Jutland. | Richard Strauss, 'Ariadne auf Naxos'. |
| | US President Woodrow Wilson is re-elected. | Film: *Intolerance.* |
| | Lloyd George becomes British Prime Minister. | |
| 1917 | First World War: | P G Wodehouse, *The Man With Two Left Feet.* |
| | Battle of Passchendaele (Third Ypres). | T S Eliot, *Prufrock and Other Observations.* |
| | British and Commonwealth forces take Jerusalem. | Film: *Easy Street.* |
| | USA declares war on Germany. | |
| | Balfour Declaration favouring the establishment of a national home for the Jewish People in Palestine. | |
| | China declares war on Germany and Russia. | |
| | German and Russian delegates sign armistice at Brest-Litovsk. | |

| YEAR | AGE | THE LIFE AND THE LAND |
|------|-----|------------------------|
| **1918** | 58 | Nov: Troops loyal to West Ukrainian Republic capture Lwów. |

4 Nov: Austrian governor decides to hand over authority to the Regency Council; a Socialist-led Provisional Government of the Republic of Poland formed.

10 Nov: Piłsudski released from Magdeburg prison and returns to Warsaw

14 Nov: Regency Council dissolves itself and hands power to Piłsudski.

18 Nov: Piłsudski forms a government

21 Dec: Piłsudski writes to Dmowski in Paris suggesting basis for future co-operation.

25 Dec: IP arrives in Danzig and proceeds to Poznań.

27 Dec: Fighting in Poznań between Polish and German communities.

| YEAR | HISTORY | CULTURE |
|------|---------|---------|
| **1918** | First World War: | Alexander Blok, *The Twelve.* |
| | Peace Treaty of Brest-Litovsk between Russia and the Central Powers. | Gerald Manley Hopkins, *Poems.* |
| | | Luigi Pirandello, *Six Characters in Search of an Author.* |
| | German Spring offensives on Western Front fail. | |
| | Romania signs Peace of Bucharest with Germany and Austria-Hungary. | |
| | Ex-Tsar Nicholas II and family executed. | |
| | Allied offensives on Western Front have German army in full retreat. | |
| | Armistice signed between Allies and Germany; German Fleet surrenders. | |
| | Kaiser Wilhelm II of German abdicates. | |

| YEAR | AGE | THE LIFE AND THE LAND |
|------|-----|------------------------|
| 1919 | 59 | Jan: Dmowski appointed first Polish delegate to Paris Peace Conference. |
| | | 2 Jan: IP arrives in Warsaw. |
| | | 17 Jan: IP appointed Prime Minister |
| | | 20 Jan: USA recognises Polish Government |
| | | 23 Jan: France recognises Polish Government |
| | | 25 Jan: Great Britain recognises Polish Government |
| | | 26 Jan: First general elections held in Poland |
| | | 27 Jan: Italy recognises Polish Government; IP Prime Minister and Minister for Foreign Affairs. |
| | | 29 Jan: Dmowski presents Polish case to Peace Conference. |
| | | 2 Apr: Paderewski arrives in Paris for Peace Conference. |
| | | 7 May: first draft of Polish-German Treaty completed |
| | | 8 May: IP leaves Paris. |
| | | 24 Jul: IP persuades Polish Sejm to ratify Polish-German Treaty |
| | | 28 Jun: IP and Dmowski sign final version of the Polish-German Treaty |
| | | 16–17 Aug: Polish Uprising in Upper Silesia. |
| | | 9 Dec: IP resigns as Prime Minister and Minister for Foreign Affairs. |

| YEAR | HISTORY | CULTURE |
|------|---------|---------|
| 1919 | Communist Revolt in Berlin. | Bauhaus movement founded by Walter Gropius. |
| | Benito Mussolini founds fascist movement in Italy. | Thomas Hardy, *Collected Poems*. |
| | British-Persian agreement at Tehran to preserve integrity of Persia. | George Bernard Shaw, *Heartbreak House*. |
| | Irish War of Independence begins. | Film: *The Cabinet of Dr Caligari*. |
| | US Senate votes against ratification of Versailles Treaty, leaving the USA outside the League of Nations. | |

| YEAR | AGE | THE LIFE AND THE LAND |
|------|-----|-----------------------|
| **1920** | 60 | Feb: IP leaves Poland for Switzerland; Polish units enter Kiev. |
| | | 25 Apr: Polish-Soviet war breaks out. |
| | | 14 May: Piłsudski authorises attack on Eastern Galicia |
| | | 18 May: Dmowski returns to Poland. |
| | | 24 May: First meeting between Dmowski and Piłsudski. |
| | | Jun: Poles forced out of Kiev by Red Army. |
| | | 28 July: Conference of Ambassadors discusses the Polish-Czechoslovak border conflict. |
| | | 6 Aug: Battle of Warsaw between Polish |
| | | 18 Aug: Soviet retreat from Warsaw begins. |
| | | 20 Aug: Second Polish uprising in Upper Silesia. |
| | | 12 Oct: Poles occupy Wilno. |
| | | 14 Dec: IP resigns as Polish delegate to international conferences. |
| **1921** | 61 | 19 Feb; Franco-Polish Alliance. |
| | | 18 Mar: Treaty of Riga defines the Polish-Soviet border. |
| | | 20 Mar: Plebiscite in Upper Silesia. |
| | | 3 May: Third Polish uprising in Upper Silesia. |
| | | 7 May: IP resigns as Polish delegate to the League of Nations. |
| **1922** | 62 | May: IP resumes playing the piano while on holiday in the United States |
| | | 4 Apr: Sejm votes for the incorporation of Wilno into Poland. |
| | | 5 Nov: General elections to the Sejm |
| | | 22 Nov: IP's first post-war concert at Carnegie Hall, New York |
| | | 16 Dec: Polish President Gabriel Narutowicz assassinated. |

| YEAR | HISTORY | CULTURE |
|------|---------|---------|
| 1920 | League of Nations comes into existence. | F Scott Fitzgerald, *This Side of Paradise.* |
| | The Hague is selected as seat of International Court of Justice. | Franz Kafka, *The Country Doctor.* |
| | League of Nations headquarters moved to Geneva. | Katherine Mansfield, *Bliss.* |
| | Warren G Harding wins US Presidential election. | |
| | Bolsheviks win Russian Civil War. | |
| | Government of Ireland Act passed. | |
| | Adolf Hitler announces his 25-point programme in Munich. | |
| 1921 | Paris Conference of wartime allies fixes Germany's reparation payments. | D H Lawrence, *Women in Love.* |
| | | John Dos Passos, *Three Soldiers.* |
| | Irish Free State established. | Prokofiev, 'The Love for Three Oranges'. |
| | Washington Naval Treaty signed. | |
| 1922 | Chanak Crisis. | T S Eliot, *The Waste Land.* |
| | Britain recognises Kingdom of Egypt under Fuad I. | James Joyce, *Ulysses.* |
| | League of Nations council approves British mandate in Palestine. | F Scott Fitzgerald, *The Beautiful and Damned.* |
| | | Film: *Dr. Mabuse the Gambler.* |

| YEAR | AGE | THE LIFE AND THE LAND |
|------|-----|-----------------------|
| **1923** | 63 | 30 Mar: Council of Ambassadors approves Poland's Eastern border. |
| | | Oct: Dmowski becomes Minister for Foreign Affairs. |
| **1926** | 66 | 12 May: Piłsudski stages *coup d'état*. |
| **1928** | 68 | 4 Mar: General elections to the Sejm |
| | | General Sikorski dismissed for his opposition to Piłsudski, contacts IP to organise opposition to the regime. |
| | | Dmowski creates new party, the National Alliance. |
| **1930** | 70 | 30 Aug: Sejm dissolved. |
| | | 16 Nov: Opposition party leaders arrested; elections to the Sejm – ruling regime secures majority. |
| **1931** | 71 | 26 Oct: Political trials of opposition leaders open. |
| **1934** | 74 | 16 Jan: Death of Helena Paderewska. |
| | | 26 Jan: Polish-German Non-Aggression Pact signed. |
| | | 13 Sep: Poland withdraws from Minority Treaties. |
| **1935** | 75 | 23 Mar: New constitution approved by the Sejm. |
| | | 12 May: Piłsudski dies. |
| | | 8 Sep: General elections to the Sejm. |
| **1936** | 76 | Opposition leaders form Morges Front at IP's house in Switzerland. |

| YEAR | HISTORY | CULTURE |
|------|---------|---------|
| 1923 | French and Belgian troops occupy the Ruhr. Adolf Hitler's *coup d'état* (The Beer Hall Putsch) fails. | P G Wodehouse, *The Inimitable Jeeves.* |
| 1926 | Germany admitted to League of Nations. | A A Milne, *Winnie the Pooh.* |
| 1928 | Transjordan becomes self-governing under the British Mandate. Kellogg-Briand Pact outlawing war and providing for peaceful settlement of disputes, is signed. | D H Lawrence, *Lady Chatterley's Lover.* |
| 1930 | The United Kingdom, France, Italy, Japan and the US sign the London Naval Treaty regulating naval expansion. | Noel Coward, *Private Lives.* Film: *All Quiet on the Western Front.* |
| 1931 | National Government formed in Great Britain. | Films: *Dracula. Little Caesar.* |
| 1934 | Germany, 'Night of the Long Knives'. Hitler becomes *Führer* of Germany. USSR admitted to League of Nations. | Robert Graves, *I, Claudius.* Shostakovich, 'Lady Macbeth of Mtsensk'. |
| 1935 | Saarland is incorporated into Germany following a plebiscite. League of Nations imposes sanctions against Italy following invasion of Abyssinia. | T S Eliot, *Murder in the Cathedral.* Films: *The 39 Steps. Top Hat.* |
| 1936 | German troops occupy Rhineland. | J M Keynes, *General Theory of Employment, Interest and Money.* |

| YEAR | AGE | THE LIFE AND THE LAND |
|------|-----|------------------------|
| **1937** | 77 | IP stars in the film *Moonlight Sonata* in which he plays an ageing pianist. The only known film of IP playing the piano. |
| **1938** | 78 | 17 Mar: Poland establishes diplomatic relations with Lithuania<br><br>2 Oct: Polish troops occupy Trans Olza region.<br><br>24 Oct: Germans demand extraterritorial link to East Prussia.<br><br>6 Nov: General elections to the Sejm. |
| **1939** | 79 | 12 Jan: Dmowski dies.<br><br>16 Feb: IP to USA for 20th tour.<br><br>31 Mar: Great Britain guarantees Polish territory.<br><br>1 Sep: Germany invades Poland.<br><br>3 Sep: Britain and France declare war on Germany.<br><br>17 Sept: Soviet Union occupies Eastern Poland.<br><br>30 Sep: Polish Government in Exile lead by Sikorski formed in Paris; IP considered for President but rejected on grounds of age. |
| **1940** | 80 | 6 Nov: IP arrives in USA from Switzerland via Portugal. |
| **1941** | 80 | 29 Jun: IP dies.<br><br>5 Jul: IP buried in Arlington cemetery. |

| YEAR | HISTORY | CULTURE |
|------|---------|---------|
| 1937 | Italy joins German–Japanese Anti-Comintern Pact. | George Orwell, *The Road to Wigan Pier*. |
| 1938 | German troops enter Austria which is declared part of the German Reich.<br><br>Munich Agreement hands Sudetenland to Germany.<br><br>Kristallnacht in Germany – Jewish houses, synagogues and schools burn for a week. | Graham Greene, *Brighton Rock*.<br>Evelyn Waugh, *Scoop*.<br>Films: *Alexander Nevsky. The Adventures of Robin Hood*. |
| 1939 | Germans troops enter Prague.<br>Italy invades Albania.<br>Spanish Civil War ends as nationalists take Madrid.<br>Pact of Steel signed by Hitler and Mussolini.<br>Nazi-Soviet pact agrees no fighting and partition of Poland: Japanese withdraw from Anti-Comintern Pact in protest.<br>Soviets invade Finland. | Bela Bartok, *String Quartet No. 6*.<br>James Joyce, *Finnegan's Wake*.<br>Thomas Mann, *Lotte in Weimar*.<br>John Steinbeck, *The Grapes of Wrath*.<br>Films: *Gone with the Wind. Goodbye Mr Chips. The Wizard of Oz*. |
| 1940 | Second World War: German conquest of Western Europe. | Ernest Hemingway, *For Whom the Bell Tolls*. |
| 1941 | Second World War.<br>Germany invades USSR | Film: *The Maltese Falcon*. |

# Bibliographical Note

Although Dmowski and Paderewski played an equally important role at the Paris Peace Conference, the former's contribution has been largely forgotten by Western historians. This may be due to the fact that they are perceived in very different ways. Dmowski was seen as an ideologue and a politician. His contribution to the development of Polish national thinking cannot be overlooked, though many of his racial theories were similar to those of the Nazis. He is less known for his diplomatic skills. Ultimately the efforts he made during the war and in Paris have been overlooked. Paderewski, on the other hand, was always a musician of international standing and that has helped to preserve his legend. Although he was unquestioningly committed to the Polish cause, his contribution to music and his lifestyle, rather than his political activities, were the subject of public attention. In a way that is easily understandable nowadays, the media focused on Paderewski in a way they did not on Dmowski. Unfortunately, he is more likely to be remembered as the pianist who went to the Peace Conference rather than as the politician who negotiated the Polish case. For both men, their participation in the Paris talks was the high point of their lives, though for

Dmowski this was the only time when he transcended the narrow milieu of Polish politics.

There is only one biography of Dmowski in English. Alvin Marcus Fountain II wrote *Roman Dmowski: Party, Tactics, Ideology 1895–1907* (East European Monographs, Boulder: 1980). The main focus of this book is the evolution of Dmowski's political ideas and it does not cover his wartime activities or the Peace Conference. Polish readers will, of course, fair better. Although Dmowski continues to be seen as a controversial figure, he cannot be ignored and so even during the Communist period a number of biographies were published. Andrzej Micewski's *Roman Dmowski* (Wydawnictwo 'Verum', Warszawa: 1971), Roman Wapiński's *Roman Dmowski* (Wydawnictwo Lubelskie, Lublin: 1988), and Krzysztof Kowalec's *Roman Dmowski* (Editions Spotkania, Warszawa: 1996) all make solid contributions. After the Second World War the Polish community in exile preserved the memory of the nationalist thinker and a number of Polish-language publications appeared abroad. Jędrzej Giertych's *Roman Dmowski, 1864–1939* (S.I.: 1947) is one example. Dmowski's admirers have made their own modest contribution to what we know of the man by publishing personal accounts. Izabella Wolikowska, whose parents were Dmowski's personal friends and whose own family became Dmowski's surrogate family wrote *Roman Dmowski, człowiek, Polak, przyjaciel* (Wydawnictwo Nortom, Wrocław: 2007). This is a very personal account, explaining his lifestyle, his character and offering glimpses into his relations with other people. Mariusz Kułakowski's two-volume *Roman Dmowski w świetle listów i wspomnień* (Gryf Publications Ltd., London: 1968) is a collection of accounts by and interviews with those who knew Dmowski personally. Dmowski's own works appeared in Polish, English and French. Though he did not write any memoirs, we have short pieces and accounts written by him and by those who knew him.

For the reasons explained above, English-language readers have a slightly better choice of books from which to gain an understanding of the tortured soul of the great musician Paderewski. Of these the most accessible is Adam Zamoyski's *Paderewski* (Collins, London, 1982). A considerably more critical biography is Marian Marek Drozdowski's *Ignacy Jan Paderewski: A Political Biography* (Interpress, Kraków: 1981). The two authors are in agreement how important Paderewski was in influencing President Wilson's policies during and after the First World War, but Zamoyski offers more details on Paderewski's personal and social life. Of the Polish language biographies, the most comprehensive is Roman Wapiński's *Ignacy Paderewski* (Ossolineum, Wrocław: 1999). Fortunately for posterity, in 1924 Mary Lawton, a journalist from the United States, approached Paderewski on behalf of a publishing house with a suggestion that he should allow her to write his biography. He agreed and over the coming years they met periodically and she took notes which she then wrote up and which Paderewski would subsequently check. The result of this long-term project was the two-volume *Paderewski Memoirs* (Collins, London: 1939). It has its limitations, however. As Paderewski was selective in what he chose to speak about – he would on the whole avoid subjects which had caused him distress – and the result is that they are of little use to those who wish to study Paderewski's contribution to the restoration of Poland to the map of Europe, as he refused to dwell on that period.

Although this book focuses primarily on the role played by Paderewski and Dmowski, it is impossible to leave Piłsudski out of the picture. His role in determining the course of events in the Polish territories during the war and his critical contribution to the establishment of the first independent Polish administration cannot be ignored. One has to understand Piłsudski's actions in order to grasp on the one hand what was being discussed and decided in Paris and on the other hand, what was actually taking place in Eastern Europe. There are two English-language biographies of Piłsudski. The earlier is M K Dziewanowski's *Jozel Pilsudski: A European federalist, 1918–1922* (Stanford: 1969), while the most up-to-date is Andrzej Garlicki's *Józef Piłsudski 1867–1935* (Scholar Press, London: 1995). Naturally, there are numerous Polish-language publications on Piłsudski, of which two stand out: Wacław Jerzejewicz's *Józef Piłsudski, 1867–1935* (Polska Fundacja Kulturalna, Londyn: 1982) and the definitive two-volume biography by Andrzej Garlicki, *Józej Piłsudski, 1867–1935* (Czytelnik, Warsaw, 1988).

The Polish question was the focus of numerous debates during the Paris Peace Conference but was also discussed in the various forums that were established after the signing of the Treaty, so the authors who wrote about the Paris talks naturally had to devote some time to explaining the Polish case. Margaret MacMillan in her *Peacemakers: The Paris Conference of 1919 and its Attempt to End War* (John Murray, London: 2002) has a good chapter on Poland. An earlier publication offers a less entertaining but nonetheless very thorough analysis of the Conference. This is F S Marston, *The Peace Conference of 1919: Organisation and Procedure* (Oxford University Press, Oxford: 1944), which places the Polish question in the context of the progress of the Conference as a whole. A focused study of the Polish case is offered by Kay Lundgreen-Neilson in *The Polish Problem at the Paris*

*Peace Conference. A study of the policies of the Great Powers and the Poles, 1918–1939* (Odense, Odense University Press: 1979). A Polish-language publication concentrating entirely on the Polish-German conflict during the talks is J Pajewski *et al* (eds), *Problem Polsko-Niemiecki w traktacie Wersalskim* (Instytut Zachodni, Poznań: 1964).

There are a number of books which address the question of the restoration of Poland in which the Paris talks form an important chapter, though the authors' studies are not generally confined to the key years of 1919–20. For a wide-ranging and thorough debate of factors which underlay the decision-making process in Paris there is no better book than Wiktor Sukiennicki, *East Central Europe During World War I: From Foreign Domination to National Independence* (East European Monographs, Boulder: 1984). Poland's post-war borders presented the Great Powers with a series of crises, drawing them into a mediatory role which they assumed only reluctantly. Titus Komarnicki's *Rebirth of the Polish Republic. A Study in the Diplomatic History of Europe, 1914–1920* (William Heinemann, London: 1957), in spite of its age, still reads well. For the post-war period see Anna Cienciala and T Komarnicki, *From Versailles to Locarno. Keys to Polish Foreign Policy 1919–1925* (Lawrence, Kansas University Press: 1984), and Paul Latawski, *The Reconstruction of Poland, 1914–23* (Macmillan, London: 1991).

Of a more general nature but still covering the period from the restoration of Poland to the present day are Jerzy Lukowski and Herbert Zawadzki, *A Concise History of Poland* (Cambridge University Press, Cambridge: 2001) and Anita J Prazmowska, *A History of Poland* (Palgrave, Basingstoke: 2004).

# Picture Sources

The author and publishers wish to express their thanks to the following sources of illustrative material and/or permission to reproduce it. They will make proper acknowledgements in future editions in the event that any omissions have occurred.

Photographs courtesy of Topham Picturepoint.

## Endpapers

*The Signing of Peace in the Hall of Mirrors, Versailles, 28th June 1919* by Sir William Orpen (Imperial War Museum: akgImages London)

Front row: Dr Johannes Bell (Germany) signing with Herr Hermann Müller leaning over him

Middle row (seated, left to right): General Tasker H Bliss, Col E M House, Mr Henry White, Mr Robert Lansing, President Woodrow Wilson (United States); M Georges Clemenceau (France); Mr David Lloyd George, Mr Andrew Bonar Law, Mr Arthur J Balfour, Viscount Milner, Mr G N Barnes (Great Britain); Prince Saionji (Japan)

Back row (left to right): M Eleftherios Venizelos (Greece);

Dr Afonso Costa (Portugal); Lord Riddell (British Press);
Sir George E Foster (Canada); M Nikola Pašić (Serbia);
M Stephen Pichon (France); Col Sir Maurice Hankey,
Mr Edwin S Montagu (Great Britain); the Maharajah of
Bikaner (India); Signor Vittorio Emanuele Orlando (Italy);
M Paul Hymans (Belgium); General Louis Botha (South
Africa); Mr W M Hughes (Australia)

## Jacket images

(Front): Imperial War Museum: akg Images.
(Back): *Peace Conference at the Quai d'Orsay* by Sir William
Orpen (Imperial War Museum: akg Images).
Left to right (seated): Signor Orlando (Italy); Mr Robert
Lansing, President Woodrow Wilson (United States); M
Georges Clemenceau (France); Mr David Lloyd George, Mr
Andrew Bonar Law, Mr Arthur J Balfour (Great Britain);
Left to right (standing): M Paul Hymans (Belgium); Mr
Eleftherios Venizelos (Greece); The Emir Feisal (The
Hashemite Kingdom); Mr W F Massey (New Zealand);
General Jan Smuts (South Africa); Col E M House (United
States); General Louis Botha (South Africa); Prince Saionji
(Japan); Mr W M Hughes (Australia); Sir Robert Borden
(Canada); Mr G N Barnes (Great Britain); M Ignacy
Paderewski (Poland)

# Index

## A

Alma-Tadema, Lawrence 9
Asquith, Herbert H 9,
    47–8
August, Zygmund viii
Austria vii, x-xiv, 3, 26, 31,
    35, 39–43, 45, 47, 52, 93,
    95
Austrian Polish Legions 71

## B

Babinski 4
Balfour, Arthur J 9, 54,
    72–3, 78
Balicki, Zygmunt 22–4
Balkans 15, 78
Baltic viii-ix, 24, 29, 39, 69,
    77, 83, 108, 112, 157
Baranowicze 111
Barringdon, Lady 8
Bartel, Kazimierz 132

Batory, Stefan (Prince of
    Transylvania) ix
Battle of Warsaw 111
Belgium xv
Belloc, Hilaire 53
Belorussia x-xi, 29, 110,
    112, 159
Białystok 110–11
Biliński, Leon 103–4
Black Sea viii, 29
Bolshevik 55, 66, 92, 126,
    155
Bosnia xxi, 34, 42
Bourne, Cardinal 47
Bowman, Dr I 79
Brest-Litovsk 39, 55–6, 68,
    93
Britain xv, xxi, 8–9, 26, 38,
    44–5, 48, 53–6, 61, 72, 76,
    79, 94, 107–8, 110–12,
    142, 152, 156, 158

Bródno 138
Brześć 147
Budenny, Semion 110
Burne-Jones, Edward 7, 9
Bytom (Beuthe) 107

## C

Cambon, Jules 79
Camp for Greater Poland
  (OWP) 133–5
Carpathian Mountains
  92
Catherine the Great ix-x
Catholic Church 13, 136–7,
  145
Cecil, Lord Robert 54
Central Lithuanian State
  113
Chorzów 107
Christian Democrats
  (Chadecja) 127
Churchill, Winston 9
Clemenceau, Georges 55,
  78–9, 86, 88–90
Commission on Polish
  Affairs 86
Congress Poland xiii, xvii,
  23–4, 47, 99, 111
Corridor 91, 103, 155
Cytadela 24
Czechoslovakia 77, 109–11,
  141–2, 151, 155–6

## D

Dąbrowa Basin 69
Dallas-Yorke, Mrs 8
Danzig 73–4, 85–6, 88–90,
  98, 100, 102–3, 111,
  141–2, 155, 158
Danzig Nazi Party 103
de Brancovan of Wallachia,
  Princess Rachel 13
della Torretta, Marquis
  79
Denikin, General Anton 94,
  108–9
Directorate of the
  Ukrainian Peoples'
  Republic 110
Dłuski, Kazimierz 80
Dmowski, Roman
  xxi–xxii, 15–16, 18–34,
  41, 44, 46–7, 53–5, 61–8,
  70, 72, 77, 80–9, 91, 93,
  95, 97, 101–2, 112, 121,
  124–39, 141, 154–5,
  186–8
Drohobycz 91
Drummond, Sir Eric 54
Duchy of Lithuania viii, 3
Duchy of Warsaw xiii

## E

East Prussia x, 38, 77, 84–5,
  88, 91, 98, 121, 155

# F

Fascists 128, 134
France ix–xv, xxi, 4, 7, 26,
    35, 44–7, 54–6, 61–3, 67,
    72, 76, 78, 80–1, 85, 94,
    107–10, 112, 114, 124,
    142, 146, 152, 156
Franco, General 153
Franz Ferdinand, Archduke
    35
Front Morges 150
Fuller-Maitland, J A 144

# G

Galicia x, 39, 41, 55, 79, 85,
    89, 91–5, 105, 108–11,
    115, 121, 125, 157, 159
Gandhi, Mahatma 152
Germany xxii, 7, 26, 28, 31,
    34, 38–42, 45, 47, 52–6,
    63, 65, 67, 74, 79, 81–2,
    85, 89–91, 93–4, 96–8,
    105–7, 110, 114, 129–30,
    136, 140, 142, 151–2,
    155 8
Gliwice (Gleiwitz) 107
Głos ('The Voice') 22
Górski 5
Grabski, Stanisław 86, 91
Grabski, Władysław 130
Great Britain 102
Grodno 92, 110–11

Grottger, Artur xix

# H

Habsburg Empire 38
Haller, General 146, 150
Hanotaux, Gabriel 153
Harmsworth, Alfred (later
    Lord Northcliffe) 10, 48
Hungary 77, 156

# I

Ichiai, K 79

# J

Jadwiga viii
Jogaila viii

# K

Katowice (Kattowitz) 107
Keynes, J M 97
Kingdom of Poland viii,
    xiii, 42, 92
Kolchak, Admiral
    Alexander 109
Kościuszko, Tadeusz xi, 64
Kraków xii, 69, 93, 188
Kuryłówka 3

# L

League of Nations 84, 90,
    96, 98, 102–3, 107, 142
Leschetizky, Theodor 6

Lithuania viii, xii, 3, 92, 109, 112, 157
Livonia x
Łódź 33
Lwów 25–6, 91, 93–4

**M**

MacDonnell, Mervyn 103
Madison Square Gardens 148
Małcużyński, Witold 147
Małopolska xii
*Manru* 13
Masovia xi-xii
Masurian Lakes 38
Matejko, Jan xix
Melba, Nellie 48
Mickewicz, Adam xviii, 14
Minority Treaty 96–7, 114
Minsk 110–11
Moraczewski, Jędrzej 80

**N**

Namier, Lewis 54, 85, 94
National Christian Movement 143
National Democratic Movement 31, 33, 71, 127
National Democratic Party xxii, 26, 28, 61, 124–5, 129–30

National League 24–5, 27–8
Nationalist Alliance (SN) 134
Nationalist movement xviii, 15, 21, 25, 127–9, 133–8, 154
National-Radical Camp (ONR) 136
Neisse 158
Nicolson, Harold 77
Niemen, River xii
Niklewicz family 138

**O**

Oder 158
Orlando, Vittorio 78–9

**P**

Pact of Non-Aggression 103
Paderewska, Antonina (nee Korsakówna) 5
Paderewska, Helena (nee Górska) 13, 87–8, 104,148–9
Paderewski, Alfred 5, 13
Paderewski, Ignacy Jan 3–18, 44, 46–9, 52, 61–8, 72–5, 77, 80, 85–91, 93–7, 99–106, 110, 131, 140–55
Pale of Settlement 30
Paris xiii-xv, 5–6, 13, 22–3, 53–4, 62, 67, 72–3, 77,

79–81, 85–6, 88–9, 91–3,
95, 99–102, 106, 108–9,
112, 124, 127, 132, 151,
154–5, 157
Paris Peace Conference
75–7, 80, 86, 88, 94,
98–9, 102, 108, 126,
139–40, 144, 146, 154–5
Partition vii-viii, x-xii, xiv,
xvii-xviii, xxii, 3–4, 6,
14, 24, 26–7, 31, 41, 99,
114
Pavlova, Anna 13
Peasant Alliance 63
Peasant Party xxii, 69, 105,
115, 125–6, 128, 131–2,
146
Peasant Party (Piast) 115,
127–8
Peasant Party (Wyzwolenie)
115
Pétain, General 152
Petlura, Semen 110
Pichon, Stephen 78, 80
Piedmont viii
Piłsudski, Józef xxi-xxii,
23, 32, 41–4, 55, 62–3,
68–73, 75, 77, 80–1, 89,
91–4, 99–101, 105–6,
108–13, 115–16, 124–6,
128–9, 131–5, 137, 141–3,
145–7, 150–2, 154, 157

Pilz, Erazm 63
Podlasie 18
Podolia xi, 3
Polish Authority 43, 92
Polish Commission 79, 84,
88, 90, 94, 108
Polish Delegation 78–9,
81–2, 86, 88, 95–7, 108,
110–11
Polish League 22, 24
Polish Legions 44, 131
Polish Liquidation
Commission 69
Polish Nation xix, 7, 16,
22, 27–30, 41, 52, 55, 64,
81–3, 85, 130, 136
Polish National Committee
(KNP) 54–5, 61–4, 66–8,
72–3, 75, 80–1, 86, 101–2
*Polish Politics and the
Rebuilding of a State* 129
Polish Romanticism xviii
Polish Socialist Party 32, 43
Polish Victims Relief Fund
47
Polish-Americans 49
Polish-Lithuanian
Commonwealth vii-x,
xii, 29, 31, 43, 48, 67, 83,
108, 112
Poniatowski, Stanisław
August ix

Poznań 74, 77, 82, 84, 91, 98, 126, 138, 155

Praga 19

Prague 27

Primate of Poland 139

Provisional Council of State of the Kingdom of Poland 42

Provisional Government of the People's Republic of Poland 70

*Przegląd Wszechpolski* 129

Puławski Legion 41, 44

Pulitzer, Joseph 12

# R

Raczkiewicz, Władysław 152

Rhineland 90

Ribbentrop-Molotov Pact 151

Riga 24, 157

Romania 7, 42, 77, 96, 151–2

Roosevelt, President 12–13, 152–3

Runowski 4

Russia vii, ix-xvi, 3, 20, 32–5, 40–5, 47, 53, 55, 72, 77, 92, 94, 106, 108–9, 111–12, 126, 129–31, 155

# S

Sejm x, 86, 94–5, 97–100, 109, 113, 115, 125, 127, 131–2, 135

Seyda, Marian 63

Sienkiewicz, Henryk xix, 12, 47

Sikorski, General Władysław 131, 146, 150–2

Silesia 55, 67, 84–5, 90–1, 98, 100, 106–7, 121, 142, 155

Słowacki, Juliusz xviii

Sobieski, Jan ix

Social Darwinist 26

Sonnino, Sidney 78

Soviet Union 109, 112, 129–30, 141–2, 151, 155, 157–9

Sowinski 4

Spa 110, 141

Stravinsky, Igor 147

# T

Tannenberg 38

Tarnopol 111

Teschen 79, 82, 89, 91, 111, 121, 142, 156

Teutonic Knights viii

*The Thinking of the Modern Pole* 27

*The Year of 1920* 129
Thugutt, Stanisław 115
Toruń xi
Treaty of Brest-Litovsk 55, 68
Treaty of Riga 111
Treaty of Tilsit xiii
Treaty of Versailles 94, 99, 129
Tukhachevsky, General Mikhail 110
Turkey 78
Tyrrell, W 79

## U

Ukraine xi, 29–30, 79, 83, 85–6, 93, 109–10, 112, 124–5, 142, 159
Union of the National and Peasant Party 126
Upper Silesia 84–5, 90–1, 100, 106–7, 142, 155

## V

Vasa ix
Vistula (Wisła) 102, 111

## W

Walewska, Marie xiii

Warsaw xii-xiii, xv, 3, 5, 16, 18–22, 24, 27, 33, 39, 42, 46, 68, 70, 72–3, 74, 79–81, 99–100, 104, 110–11, 113, 124–7, 138–9, 145, 149
Wielkopolska xi
Wilno (Vilnius) 92–3, 110–13, 156
Wilson, President Woodrow 45, 49, 50–3, 55–6, 65, 75, 78–9, 88–90, 95–6, 102
Witos, Wincenty 69, 105, 115, 125, 127–31, 146, 150

## Y

Yudenich, General Nikolai 109

## Z

Zamoyski, Maurycy 63
Zbrucz, river 92, 111
Żeligowski, General Lucjan 113
Żeromski, Stefan xx
ZET 20–1
Zhytomir 111

# Makers of the Modern World

UK PUBLICATION: November 2008 to December 2010
CLASSIFICATION: Biography/History/
    International Relations
FORMAT: 198 × 128mm
EXTENT: 208pp
ILLUSTRATIONS: 6 photographs plus 4 maps
TERRITORY: world

Chronology of life in context, full index, bibliography innovative layout with sidebars

*Woodrow Wilson: United States of America* by Brian Morton
*Friedrich Ebert: Germany* by Harry Harmer
*Georges Clemenceau: France* by David Watson
*David Lloyd George: Great Britain* by Alan Sharp
*Prince Saionji: Japan* by Jonathan Clements
*Wellington Koo: China* by Jonathan Clements
*Eleftherios Venizelos: Greece* by Andrew Dalby
*From the Sultan to Atatürk: Turkey* by Andrew Mango
*The Hashemites: The Dream of Arabia* by Robert McNamara
*Chaim Weizmann: The Dream of Zion* by Tom Fraser
*Piip, Meierovics & Voldemaras: Estonia, Latvia & Lithuania* by Charlotte Alston
*Ignacy Paderewski: Poland* by Anita Prazmowska
*Beneš, Masaryk: Czechoslovakia* by Peter Neville
*Károlyi & Bethlen: Hungary* by Bryan Cartledge
*Karl Renner: Austria* by Jamie Bulloch
*Vittorio Orlando: Italy* by Spencer Di Scala
*Pašić & Trumbić: The Kingdom of Serbs, Croats and Slovenes* by Dejan Djokic
*Aleksandŭr Stamboliĭski: Bulgaria* by R J Crampton
*Ion Bratianu: Romania* by Keith Hitchin
*Paul Hymans: Belgium* by Sally Marks
*General Smuts: South Africa* by Antony Lentin
*William Hughes: Australia* by Carl Bridge
*William Massey: New Zealand* by James Watson
*Sir Robert Borden: Canada* by Martin Thornton
*Maharajah of Bikaner: India* by Hugh Purcell
*Afonso Costa: Portugal* by Filipe Ribeiro de Meneses
*Epitácio Pessoa: Brazil* by Michael Streeter
*South America* by Michael Streeter
*Central America* by Michael Streeter
*South East Asia* by Andrew Dalby
*The League of Nations* by Ruth Henig
*Consequences of Peace: The Versailles Settlement – Aftermath and Legacy*
    by Alan Sharp